Heuchera, Tiarella and Heucherella

A gardener's guide

Charles and Martha Oliver

Heuchera, Tiarella and Heucherella

A gardener's guide

B T Batsford

First published 2006

ISBN-13: 978 0 7134 9009 1
ISBN-10: 0 7134 9009 8

A CIP catalogue record for this book is available from the British Library.

Printed in Singapore
for the publisher
B T Batsford
The Chrysalis Building
Bramley Road
London W10 6SP

Distributed in the United States and Canada by
Sterling Publishing Co., 387 Park Avenue South,
New York, NY 10016, USA

Acknowledgements

We are grateful to Rick Mercer and Kary Arimoto-Mercer for being our hosts and guides on our California trip and to Kary for letting us use the photos she took. We thank our friend Cindy Gaulin for showing us the Santa Barbara Botanic Garden. Luc Klinkhamer introduced us to the world of international plant commerce and let us use a photo. Elizabeth Wells provided helpful information. We thank all those others who let us use photos for the book: Iza Goroff, Regina Birchem, Tom Chester (photos at http://tchester.org/sgm/plants/pix/heuchera_elegans.html), Blooms of Bressingham, and Dan Heims. The rest of the photos were taken by Charles Oliver at or near The Primrose Path nursery in Scottdale, Pennsylvania unless otherwise noted. The figures are by Martha and Charles Oliver.

Contents

Introduction

Garden hybrids of heucheras (known as coral bells or alum roots) are spectacular plants, which is surprising since their ancestors are not conspicuous, well-known wildflowers. Native to North America, they occur mostly in hills and mountains, inhabiting rocky slopes, cliffs and summits. They come in a wide array of shapes and sizes, from tiny alpines only a few centimetres high to woodland plants over 1m (3½ft) tall.

Only a few of the species are grown as garden plants since most are not very interesting in their wild forms, but the species do have some very interesting traits. A small number have showy flowers, some have silvery markings on the foliage, one or two have rare variants with purple leaves through the growing season, and a couple have forms with ruffled leaves. Plant breeders have managed to combine these disparate traits into showy garden plants that look quite unlike their ancestral wild forms.

There are about 35–50 wild species of *Heuchera*, depending on which authority you consult; 35 are currently recognized on the PLANTS Database of the US Natural Resources Conservation Service (http://plants.usda.gov). They belong to the family Saxifragaceae, and are herbaceous perennials that grow as clumps of leaves arising from central crowns held just above the surface of the ground. The leaves may be rounded or lobed like those of maple trees, and are borne on slim petioles. Wands of small flowers rise above the foliage in late spring or summer which may be erect or arch to the sides.

There are also several genera that are closely related to *Heuchera*, being generally similar in appearance but less familiar to the general gardener. *Tiarella* (foam flower), consists of a few species found in the woodlands of North America and east Asia. They have some garden importance since the wild species show interesting differences in leaf coloration and

shape, and in the flowers. As in the case of heuchera, breeders have recently combined these traits to make a new group of garden plants quite different from any of the wild forms. Though heucheras and tiarellas do not appear to hybridize in nature, they have been crossed by breeders to produce a group of plants called *Heucherella* (foamy bells). They combine many of the traits of *Heuchera* with those of *Tiarella*, making very unusual and beautiful plants. *Mitella* (bishop's cap or mitrewort) which consists of a few species found in the woodlands of North America and east Asia, is fairly obscure, and probably of interest mainly to wildflower gardeners, while *Tellima* (fringe cups), is a single species from the Pacific Coast region of North America.

OVERVIEW OF HEUCHERA, TIARELLA AND HEUCHERELLA

Geography

The authorities recognize seven or more species of *Heuchera* in the eastern United States, but the genus taxonomy is still not settled since there seems to be natural hybridization and intergradation between the different species.

Several of the eastern species have been very important in the development of the group as garden plants. *H. americana*, an especially adaptable species, has a wide range from Connecticut and southern Ontario to Georgia and eastern Oklahoma, and inhabits rocky slopes and woodlands in a variety of soil types. *H. pubescens* has a more limited range in the Appalachians from central Pennsylvania to North Carolina, growing on rocks and cliffs. *H. alba* has a very small range in the highest mountains of West Virginia and Virginia. *H. richardsonii* is a prairie species, found from Michigan to Alberta. These species and a couple of others (*H. longiflora* and

Habitat of *Heuchera pubescens* in Greenland Gap, West Virginia

H. caroliniana) that are not ancestors of garden forms and which are unknown to the gardening public, are referred to as spring-flowering heucheras, since they flower from April into July, depending on the local climate. Two other eastern heucheras, *H. villosa* and *H. parviflora*, are referred to as the summer-flowering heucheras and are found on rocky, wooded slopes from West Virginia to Arkansas. They flower from early summer into autumn. *H. villosa* is often grown as a garden plant, but it is most important as an ancestor of many of the modern hybrids.

In the West of the USA there is more variety in the other 27 or more species of *Heuchera*, but the flowering season classification of the eastern forms does not really apply because of the climatic differences. Western heucheras are found from Alaska south to the mountains of Mexico, with the greatest diversity of species in the mountains from southern British Columbia to Arizona. Most species are small- to medium-sized plants found on cliffs and rocks.

A few of the showiest alpine species are grown by rock gardeners, but in general the western forms are not adaptable enough for general garden use. Some of the western species have been important in the history of garden heucheras though. *H. micrantha* and

H. cylindrica from the mountains of the Northwest, *H. hallii* and *H. pulchella* from the southern Rockies, *H. sanguinea* from Arizona, and *H. elegans*, *H. hirsutissima* and *H. maxima* from California have all been used by breeders to shape modern garden hybrids.

There is uncertainty, too, in how many species of *Tiarella* should be recognized. In eastern North America *T. cordifolia* grows as a woodland wildflower from New Brunswick and Michigan to the southern Appalachians. In the uplands of the Southeast there are forms often referred to as *T. wherryi* and *T. collina*, but they are now usually included under *T. cordifolia*, currently as var. *collina*. *The Flora of the Carolinas, Virginia, and Georgia* (Weakley, 2005), however, treats *T. wherryi* as a separate species. The tiarellas are part of the ephemeral spring flora of the eastern deciduous forests, flowering in the sun on the woodland floor before the trees' leaves appear, casting them in heavy shade. On the Pacific Coast *T. trifoliata* and *T. unifoliata* (often combined under the former name) grow in evergreen coniferous forests, where they flower in the summer. All these forms have been combined in the modern garden tiarella hybrids. Each has contributed special traits, and the combinations seen in the garden hybrids do not occur in nature. An additional species, *T. polyphylla*, occurs in eastern Asia but has not been used to any extent horticulturally.

Diversity of forms

Variation in heucheras and related plants consists mostly of differences in size, proportions and colour. These differences have arisen as adaptations to habitat and to methods of pollination.

Woodland types are the largest. Clumps of foliage may be 60cm (2ft) across and individual leaves 15–20cm (6–8in) wide, which gives the foliage good exposure to dim forest light. Some individuals have leaves with a slightly wavy surface, producing a greater area for light absorption without increasing the overall width of the leaf. The woodland

Habitat of *Heuchera elegans* in San Gabriel Mountains, California (photo by Tom Chester)

species have very small flowers that are borne on wiry stems 1m (3½ft) or more tall. The stem length sends the flowers above the surrounding vegetation, and the arrangement of the flowers in open sprays is an adaptation for pollination by small flies.

Species found in more open habitats grow in rocky areas and cliff crevices. The overall plant size is smaller, and in shady sites some forms may have heavily ruffled leaves. The flowers may be tiny and be borne above the foliage in open 'puffs' to attract small flies, or they may be larger and in open sprays to attract large flies and bees. Some flowers are comparatively large and brightly coloured to attract bees and hummingbirds.

The plants are most compact where climatic conditions are harsh and high winds occur, and true alpines from western North America can be very small. Flower stems are as short as a few centimetres but, with bees and hummingbirds available as pollinators, the flowers may be as large and showy as in lowland forms though the foliage may be reduced to rosettes of small, overlapping leaves. The compact growth protects the foliage from damage by high winds, pounding hail and snow, and the bright sun means that even reduced amounts of exposed foliage will produce enough food. Also, the low humidity ensures that the foliage will not stay wet so long after the summer rains that fungus diseases are a problem. The foliage of the western species is usually plain green, while the eastern spring-flowering species often have some maroon colouring along the leaf veins, and silvery grey patches between the veins on the upper side of the leaf.

Tiarellas are much more limited in diversity. All forms inhabit woodlands and are generally similar in overall size, with one important difference being the flowering time, as mentioned. But among the eastern tiarellas there are differences in growth habit, leaf shape and colour, and flower appearance. Typical *T. cordifolia*, as found in the northern part of the range, runs to create ground cover. The maple-shaped leaves are usually plain green, but sometimes there are maroon markings along the veins on the upper side of the leaf. Occasionally this is quite extensive, taking up more than half the leaf surface. The white or pale pink flowers are small and starry, and appear in an open spike. Although the individual spikes are thin and borne sparsely, when the plant has formed a mat of foliage the flowers can be very attractive making an area of white 'foam'.

In the US Southeast there are non-running forms that make more substantial clumps, with many erect stems of flowers borne more densely on the stalk. The flowers are often an attractive pink and sometimes sweetly scented; the leaf and flower stalks may be contrastingly dark, and the leaves may have a central maroon medallion and be deeply lobed. The western forms have relatively sparse, smaller white flowers on longer, more spreading stems. Their foliage is plain green but sometimes deeply lobed, even to the extent of producing separate leaflets. The single species of east Asia has flowers similar to those of western tiarellas.

The rounded leaves may have dark veining, and the leaves and flower stalks may be contrastingly dark.

The small satellite genera also have relatively little diversity. *Tellima* has occasional wild forms with silvery markings on the upper sides of the leaves. The flowers vary from greenish-white to pinkish, and some forms may be scented.

Mitellas vary in size from the relatively large and tiarella-like *M. diphylla* of the woodlands of eastern North America to the small, inconspicuous species of the West. *M. diphylla* has plain green foliage and small but attractive white flowers, and flowers with other ephemeral spring wildflowers in deciduous forests; western species inhabit coniferous forests and are spindly plants with tiny green flowers. In east Asia there are more promising species with purple flowers, and tight clumps of foliage marked on the upper sides with silvery grey or maroon.

SUITABILITY AS GARDEN PLANTS

What makes a good garden plant? As gardeners have selected plants, bringing them into cultivation, there seems to be little consensus on this issue, but generally people seem to choose plants if they are pleasing in size and shape, eyeing them with an unconscious set of criteria based on long-term human experience of looking at plants, both as food items and ornamentals.

A plant that shoots up a tall, lanky flower stalk, topping it with tiny flowers, just won't pass muster, because the proportions aren't 'right'. At the other end of the scale, tiny alpine jewels with enormous flowers in proportion to their foliage rosette are delightful, but the difficulties in growing them daunt many prospective rock gardeners. In between there seems to be an area where the shape and size pleases, and the heuchera group falls into that area, as do many other plants judged 'garden-worthy'.

The ratio of the flower stalk height to the width of the foliage clump seems to be critical,

Proportions of plants for garden use: A. too tall and lanky, B. pleasing ratio of height to width, C. alpine growth proportions.

A   B   C

with many plants (e.g. delphiniums, hollyhocks and foxgloves) falling into the 2:1–4:1 category. Of course a border with identical flower stalk to foliage ratios would be dismayingly boring, and the ability to vary things is what sets great gardeners apart from the mediocre.

The proportions of many of the heuchera/tiarella group fall into this 'pleasing' ratio, which is why they have been used for over a century as garden plants. Recently, new foliage colours have been added by hybridizers, although the selected colours do belong to the species. The vibrant purple leaves and silvery mottling were present in the wild species, especially *H. villosa* and *H. pubescens*, and the maroon veining of tiarella

hybrids can be spotted in the wild *T. cordifolia*. It was simply a matter of getting these qualities into and combining them in the hybrids, and then launching a selective breeding programme.

But garden-worthiness doesn't stop here. These plants offer a trait which sets them apart from other garden plants, and that is their year-round interest. At their best they offer deep maroon leaves over winter in contrast to the major players such as hostas, absent for six months of the year in Zone 6, and ferns, whose emerging heads are a sign of spring. Hellebores offer a winter presence but they generally remain green all season, whereas the heucheras maintain a set of mature leaves even as the new growth emerges in spring. They are initially dark (perhaps to catch a bit of heat from the sun) but become increasingly lighter, each leaf declaring itself, adding to the show.

These long-lived perennials have managed to survive heat and drought in summer, and bitter winter cold because they are native to challenging sites, namely rocky cliffs and crevices where moisture is scarce and competition for nutrients is high. In fact, failure in the garden is more often the result of overly moist conditions than any other factor (which is why it's sometimes important to add gravel or horticultural sand to the soil to improve the drainage). But if your garden has dreaded areas of 'dry shade' these plants will thrive, for example under shallow-rooted trees where astilbes and astrantias give up. The roots of deciduous trees can certainly be an asset, creating suitable conditions for small bulbs and ferns, while making life very difficult for weeds.

The flowering times of heucheras can range from mid-spring (*H.* 'Coral Bouquet' and *Tiarella* 'Elizabeth Oliver') to late spring (*H.* 'Regina' and *T.* 'Pink Brushes') to early summer (*H.* 'Quilters' Joy' and Montrose Ruby), and even to late summer (*H.* 'Frosted Violet' and 'Bronze Wave'.) It's therefore possible to arrange a sequence of flowers, all accompanied by outstanding leaves, offering good prospects for the flower arranger (yes, they make splendid cut flowers, and the leaves last even longer in a vase). But cutting off the flowers, as recommended for some of the earlier hybrids, isn't necessary with the newer large-flowered hybrids. Of course we aren't talking about flowers the size of dahlias; the newer forms have flowers as large or larger than *Convallaria* (lily-of-the-valley) which make a good display from quite a distance.

Hostas have dominated shady areas since their introduction in the 1750s, and their green or blue or striped leaves are the backbone of many a scheme. The flowers can be quite nice too, albeit appearing only in white, lavender or purple. In our garden the main drawback is the late spring frosts which often damage the new leaves, so loved by deer

Wild *Tiarella cordifolia* in Pennsylvania.

and rabbits. Of course starving deer eat anything, even toxic plants such as *Kalmia* and *Aconitum* (aconite), but generally speaking the heucheras don't appeal to them. The hairy, bitter leaves are astringent, and country people originally called *H. americana* 'Alum Root' for its ability to crisp pickles and draw wounds together, and all the wild forms seem to share this characteristic. Putting a fresh leaf in your mouth gives the sensation of a dry martini, which can't be much fun for hungry deer. That's why the leaves aren't usually touched by the herds that wander through our yard each evening (we can hear them snorting from the front porch), but we have heard of gardeners reporting nibbling after the deer finished off the hostas.

So, everything considered, heucheras and their related tiarellas offer a lot to gardeners with a woodland or shady site. The explosion of new hybrids in the last 15 years makes them eminently collectible, and the variety of new leaf colours and flower sizes increases their uses. These are plants to be reckoned with.

1 Structure and growth of heucheras and related plants

Heucheras and their relatives grow as rosettes with the foliage arising as a clump from near ground level, making a circle around a central crown, or caudex. The caudex is a short stem around which the growth buds are arranged in a spiral. Typically, one turn of the spiral bears about six leaves, the petioles overlapping like the scales of a pine cone. At the axil of each petiole is a vegetative bud capable of forming a new rosette. In addition to the flower stem, or inflorescence, buds are borne in some of the axils. At the base of the caudex, heucheras have thick, tough, branching roots capable of penetrating deeply into crevices or rocky soil. The other genera have fibrous roots more suitable to soft woodland soil.

PLANT GROWTH THROUGH THE SEASON

The plants of this group are evergreen. In autumn the foliage of many species flattens to the ground, and may turn bronzy or red-purple. In the spring there is a flush of new leaf growth which may be suffused with purple, and is usually very frost-tolerant. In almost all the wild species in this group inflorescence buds develop during the summer, and chilling during the winter provides the stimulus for flowering the following spring. A few heucheras are summer-flowering, and their inflorescence buds develop during the spring, but most species flower in mid- to late spring.

The inflorescences of early-flowering tiarellas are frost-tolerant to some degree, but those of heucheras opening in late spring are usually tender. Flowering length is usually about three to six weeks, though this is variable since there is a succession of flower buds opening on each inflorescence, and vigorous plants may send up a succession of inflorescences.

The seed ripens by mid- to late summer, and is carried in a dry capsule. When ripe it is scattered by any disturbance of the dried inflorescence. Seed that ripens early and happens to land in a favourable site may germinate that same summer, but probably most seed is scattered late in the season and germinates the following spring.

During summer, some of the vegetative axillary buds at the base of the plant rosette begin growth. By early autumn they will have formed offset crowns which put out their own roots, and the main clump becomes larger. A few species make above-ground runners which bear vegetative buds and root down to form new plants, or they make underground stolons which form new plants at their tips at some distance from the parent. They can form carpets rather than the clumps of foliage characteristic of most members of this group.

FOLIAGE

A leaf consists of three parts. The blade is the outermost part and is typically cordate, with 5–7 quite well defined lobes, separated by indentations, or sinuses. The lobes may be rounded or acute, with a varying degree of development of teeth on their margins. In a few cases the blades may be deeply lobed, even to the point of producing separate leaflets. The surface of the blade may be flat or waved.

Tissue structure within the blade may be modified to produce a silvery, reflective appearance, and the colour of the upper and lower surfaces may be green, a shade of red or purple. The petioles vary greatly in length, but generally are in proportion to the size of the blade. Petiole coloration is usually similar to that of the surface of the caudex and the underside of the blade. Where the petiole

The parts of the crown of a heuchera plant.

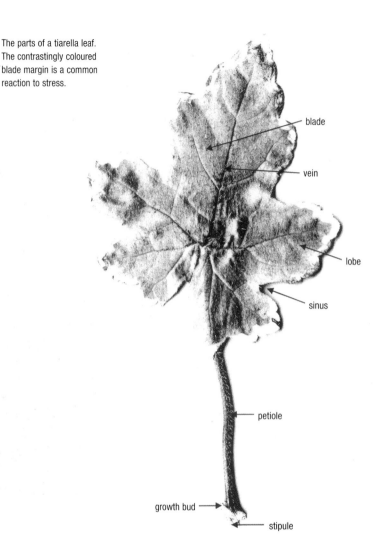

The parts of a tiarella leaf. The contrastingly coloured blade margin is a common reaction to stress.

blade

vein

lobe

sinus

petiole

growth bud

stipule

meets the caudex there are paired, ear-like structures called stipules that form a protective cover over the axillary buds.

In this group the whole plant, especially the leaves, is covered by small hairs. They may be so small and sparse that the plant appears to be smooth unless viewed under magnification, or large and dense enough to produce a rough texture or a furry appearance.

INFLORESCENCE

The peduncle arises from a leaf axil at about a 60° angle, and may then rise perpendicular or arch to one side. Along the length of the peduncle there are usually several small leaves, or bracts, of variable size. The flower branches arise one third to three quarters of the way along the length of the inflorescence, and each branch may divide in turn to bear up to 12 or 13 flower buds per primary branch. Each inflorescence may bear up to 30 or so branches and have a shape that varies from a loose, irregular spray to an even cone or cylinder.

The peduncle and stems of the flower branches are usually the same colour as the petioles, varying from grey-green to reddish or dark purple. Vigorous plants producing a

A   B   C

Flower panicles of A. heuchera, B. tiarella, C. mitella, showing the degree of division of the branches

succession of inflorescences during the season may bear hundreds or, in heucheras, thousands of flowers. Tiarellas have flower branches that usually bear only 1–2 flowers, and may form a tight cylindrical brush or an irregular spray. In the case of *Tellima* and *Mitella*, the flowers are borne singly in the inflorescence on a long, narrow spike.

FLOWERS

Heuchera flowers vary tremendously in size and structure. The basic form is campanulate, or bell-like. Rather than having all parts of the flower arise from the centre of the flower, as is usual, the lower parts of the calyx, petals, and anthers are all fused into a structure called the hypanthium.

The calyx forms a five-lobed bell. At the base of each lobe division a small, strap-like or spoon-shaped petal is attached, and the petals may project past the mouth of the bell. At the base of each lobe a stamen is attached, and these may also be exserted, i.e. project out of the flower. Also, two styles arise from the centre of the flower base, and they too may project from the calyx opening.

The smallest heuchera flowers are only

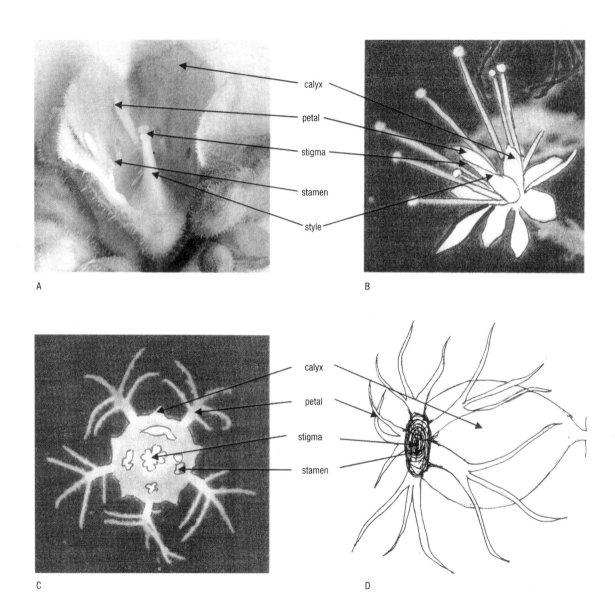

The parts of a flower of A. heuchera, B. tiarella, C. mitella, D. tellima

Seed capsules of tiarella (left) and heuchera (right).

several millimetres across, with the calyx and hypanthium reduced to a low ridge around the flower centre. Most species have flowers with calyces in the shape of a deep bowl or straight-sided bell 4–5mm (0.15–0.19in) across, and 4–6mm (0.15–0.2in) long. The largest-flowering species have straight-sided calyces up to 7mm (0.3in) across and 1.3cm (0.5in) long, or calyces flared like a trumpet at the opening and 10mm (0.4in) or so long.

The flowers of some of the large-flowered species are zygomorphic (longer on one side than another), and are borne hanging so that the opening of the calyx is held level. Other species may present the flowers facing outwards, or in no regular pattern (but the flowers do not usually have the opening face upward). Nectar accumulates around the base of the ovaries, and may form relatively large puddles in types that are pollinated by hummingbirds and large bees. The outside of the calyx bears glandular hairs, which have swollen tips and often secrete a sticky substance. The hairs may be of a contrasting colour and, to the naked eye, produce a visual appearance of colour shading. After pollination the ovary and styles grow into a two-beaked, dry capsule that eventually splits open between the styles.

Tiarella flowers are quite different. They resemble small, star-like crowns about 5mm (0.19in) across with the calyx deeply lobed, and with a separate paddle-shaped petal between each pair of lobes. There are ten stamens forming a circle around the paired styles, only one of which is functional and tipped by a stigma. After pollination the ovary forms a two-part structure, resembling a scoop whose top is partially closed by a shorter leaf. When the mature scoop is disturbed, the seeds scatter.

The calyx found in the flowers of mitellas are greatly reduced, but the five petals are enlarged and finely branched, giving each flower the appearance of a snowflake. There may be five or ten stamens. The ovary opens before the seed is ripe, and the seed grows exposed on the surface of the ovary, falling from the flower when mature. Tellimas have a cup-like calyx, but the petals resemble those of mitellas, and there are ten stamens. After pollination the ovary forms a dry capsule, from which the seeds are shaken when they are ripe. Note that seeds of the heuchera group are black and long oval, about 0.4–1mm (0.015–0.04in) long. They often bear long or short spines, but may also be spineless, with some surface sculpting.

2 Heucheras and related plants for the garden

What follows is a survey of the garden-worthy heucheras, giving readers some background about the species and cultivars on sale at nurseries, listed in mail-order catalogues and encountered in gardens. We have not attempted to make a complete list of heuchera cultivars. Many of the older ones are no longer in general circulation, and where there is a large group of similar forms, we have discussed only the ones that are most likely to be easily available and with which we are familiar. We have selected from this large list a smaller group, indicated by an asterisk next to the first use of the plant name, that we will go on to consider for garden use in much more detail in Chapter 3.

A note on nomenclature

We have tried to be consistent in using a style similar to that of the Royal Horticultural Society throughout the book. Latin species names are italicized, cultivars are within single quotes, seed strains lack the single quotes, and botanical forms are italicized, being preceded by 'f'. Sometimes it is difficult to decide on the best usage. Commercial nursery usage often differs from ours, and the names encountered in catalogues and nurseries may not be quite the same. Also note that the first use of a plant name in this chapter is in bold for ease in scanning the list. And when a genus name is used like a common name in the text, it is not italicized or capitalized.

HEUCHERAS BY CATEGORY

We have divided heucheras into five categories or series of species and cultivars, depending on the best way that they are used in the garden. When flower size is mentioned, these are the measurements that we associate with descriptive size terms. So ...

- tiny – less than 3mm (0.1in) long
- small – 3–4mm (0.1–0.15in) long
- medium – 5–7mm (0.19–0.3in) long
- large – 8–9mm (0.3–0.35in) long
- very large – over 10mm (0.4in) long.

Leaf colour descriptions are of the upper surface unless otherwise noted. There is a large environmental component in the colour and size of heuchera foliage, and readers should not be too concerned (at least at first) if a labelled, purchased plant does not exactly fit the description.

Alpine types

The size of the plants makes them suitable for use as 'alpines' in the horticultural sense. The forms include many of the small species from the mountains of western North America. Some are true alpines, inhabiting rocky places above the tree line, but many are found on cliffs and among rocks lower down. The growth habit of most is mat-forming, with the foliage in overlapping rosettes 3–10cm (1¼–4in) high, and in several years a plant may grow to a size of 20–30cm (8–12in) across, filling spaces among rocks in a very attractive manner.

Alpine forms usually flower a couple of weeks earlier than the large border types. Many of the wild species have been shy to flower for us, as Western alpines often are in eastern North America, but all of the forms we list here have been easy to grow and hardy in western Pennsylvania. The smallest heucheras are especially well suited for growing in troughs since they are crevice-dwellers, or like raised rock garden beds, and would be lost in an open garden setting. Many of the small

Heuchera grossulariifolia

wild forms can be found at alpine nurseries, or can be grown from seed from rock garden seed exchanges or from North American native seed suppliers.

H. hallii, from the Pikes Peak region of Colorado, has smooth, dark green, toothed leaves about 3cm (1¼in) across and 6–7mm (0.2–0.3in) long globular white flowers in loose sprays on 15–20cm (6–8in) long stems.

H. pulchella*, from cliffs in the mountains of central New Mexico, is well named, since good forms are very pretty. The pink flowers, on 25cm (10in) long stems, are narrow and about 5mm (0.19in) long. The smooth leaves are about 3cm (1¼in) across.

The **SanPico hybrids** were a group of crosses between *H. hallii* and *H. pulchella* made at The Primrose Path in the early 1990s. 'SanPico Rosita' was the selected cultivar from this group, and had foliage similar to that of the parents and light pink bell flowers to 20cm (8in) high. It has been lost at the nursery but is probably extant in gardens.

The **Petite Series** is a set of crosses between 'SanPico Rosita' and the full-sized *H.* 'Regina'. There are five cultivars that keep to alpine size when grown in lean soil, three with bronze and silver foliage – '**Petite Pearl Fairy**'*, '**Petite Marbled Burgundy**'* and '**Petite Ruby Frills**' – and two with green and silver foliage – '**Petite Lime Sherbet**' and '**Petite Pink Bouquet**'. All have pink flowers to about 25–30cm (10–12in). In rich soil 'Petite Marbled Burgundy' becomes considerably larger, reaching about 45cm (18in) high, and can be used in the border.

'**Mayfair**' is a hybrid between *H. hallii* and a Brizoides made by Marcel LePiniec of Mayfair Nursery in New Jersey. It has green foliage and coral-pink flowers; to 30cm (12in) high.

Heuchera abramsii

'**Constance**' is a miniature hybrid with green foliage and pink flowers to 20cm (8in) high. This was bred by Betty Ann Addison, and introduced by Rice Creek Gardens in Minnesota in 1996.

H. merriamii, from California and Oregon, has slightly hairy leaves about 3.5cm (1½in) across, and small, 4mm (0.15in) long, globular, greenish-white flowers on 15cm (6in) long stems. 'Primrose Path Selection' is a plant we picked out from a group of seedlings, and has nearly white flowers.

H. grossulariifolia, from north-western North America, has clustered, white tubular flowers to 7mm (0.3in) long. The plants we have grown are small forms with 15–20cm (6–8in) long flower stems. The leaves are smooth and dark-green, 2.5cm (1in) across and lobed like those of *Ribes grossularia*, a gooseberry. We have seen larger forms in Washington State. They looked quite attractive, and had 40cm (16in) long flower stems arching out from cliff crevices. *H. cylindrica* **var. alpina** is similar to *H. grossulariifolia* but less attractive. The leaves are slightly hairy and 2.5cm (1in) across; the flowers are greenish-white, about 6mm (0.2in) long, and borne in tight clusters on 25cm (10in) long stems.

H. alpestris, from southern California, and **H. rubescens**, which has many varieties in a wide range across the West, are among the smallest of the genus. Our *H. alpestris* has light pinkish flowers similar to those of *H. pulchella*, but a little narrower at about 4mm (0.15in) long, and leaves about 15mm (0.6in) across in a mat about 4cm (1¾in) high. *H. rubescens* varies from tiny forms with foliage only 4cm (1¾in) or so high, and flowers to 12cm (4½in) to larger forms with flowers to 40cm (16in) high. Flowers are 3–5mm (0.1–0.19in) long and greenish-white to pinkish, with recurved white petals. '**Troy Boy**'*, from the mountains of Nevada, is a very small and attractive *H. rubescens* selection. **H. rubescens var. versicolor**, from moist, shaded cliffs in the Rockies, has 4mm (0.15in) pinkish flowers and leaves 5–7cm (2–2¾in) wide. Our plants

had flower stems to about 50cm (20in) long, but there are reportedly much smaller alpine forms that would be more desirable.

In the mountains of southern California there is a group of very pretty species, all making open mats of slightly hairy foliage. All have been hardy for us, and they flower well among rocks in a raised bed. They have narrow, tubular flowers in open, airy panicles. The petals project from the calyx and are recurved, producing a frilly look. **H. parishii** is the least showy, with 5mm (0.19in) pinkish flowers on stems to about 15cm (6in) long. '**Chiquita**' is a dwarf form of this, 8cm (3½in) tall in flower from the Rancho Santa Ana Botanic Garden. **H. abramsii** has 5mm (0.19in) flowers with pink calyces and white petals to 15–17cm (6–6½in). **H. elegans*** has 6–7mm (0.2–0.3in) long flowers with

Heuchera parvifolia var. *nivalis* in Colorado Rockies

Heuchera cylindrica in the Bighorn Mountains, Wyoming. (Photo by Iza Goroff)

bicoloured pink and white calyces, and white petals; the flower stems are about 25cm (10in) tall. **H. elegans** 'Bella Blanca' is a selection with white flowers introduced by the Rancho Santa Ana Botanic Garden. **H. hirsutissima** has 6–7mm (0.2–0.3in) flowers with pink calyces and white petals on 25cm (10in) long stems. **H. hirsutissima** 'Santa Rosa'*, a selection made by Ted Kipping, has good dark pink and white flowers. This is the only heuchera with sweet-scented flowers that we have encountered.

Dara Emery at the Santa Barbara Botanic Garden in California made the **Canyon Series*** of hybrids between some of the California species and *sanguinea* hybrids (presumably = Brizoides; see Chapter 5). The smaller selections, '**Blushing Bells**', '**Canyon Chimes**', '**Dainty Bells**' and '**Pink Wave**' fit into this group of alpines as far as garden use is concerned. This series of hybrids doesn't seem to have been widely grown outside Southern California, but with suitable siting and cultivation should be hardy in the northern US, southern Canada, and Europe.

Other small montane species are more interesting than beautiful, mainly appealing to plant collectors. **H. glabra** inhabits rock crevices in the mountains from Oregon to Alaska, and has tiny whitish flowers on wiry stems to 30cm (12in) long. It is an appealing plant when seen on rocky outcrops in the spectacular settings of the Cascade Range and the Olympic Mountains, but did not last long for us in cultivation. **H. parvifolia** has a wide range in the Rockies, and we have seen **var. nivalis** nestled among rocks above the tree line at about 3400m (11,200ft) in Colorado. Despite its name the leaves are about 3.5cm (1½in) across and the tiny green flowers are borne on stems up to 30cm (12in) tall. **H. bracteata** is another Rocky Mountain species with smooth oval leaves and small green flowers on stems about 40cm (16in) or so long. There are other small species that we have not been able to obtain, but which sound interesting and might be worth growing (e.g. *H. duranii* and *H. glomerulata*).

Other rock garden heucheras

This category refers to plants that are too large to be considered alpines, but which prefer soil with sharper drainage than the types suited to the border. In the north-eastern US and southern Canada all these plants grow best with some protection from hot sun, for example on a north slope, in light tree shade, or behind a large rock. The wild plants listed here will have to be grown from seed lists or sought at specialist nurseries.

The larger members of the **Canyon hybrids*** from the Santa Barbara Botanic Garden are medium-size coral bells suitable for the rock garden. They are derived from the same group of species as the smaller Canyon hybrids, but are about twice the size. '**Canyon Pink**', '**Canyon Delight**' and '**Canyon Duet**' are all well suited to open garden use.

'**Coral Bouquet**'* is a hybrid of ours between *H. cylindrica* var. *alpina* and *H.* 'Chatterbox', a Brizoides cultivar. This has a compact tuft of silver-marked green foliage and very large coral-pink flowers in dense panicles at the top of 45–55cm (18–22in) high stems. It flowers early, like the alpine types, and retains its flowers for a long time. '**Chiqui**'* is a hybrid by George Schenk and has similar parentage. It has hairier leaves and equally large, narrower shrimp-pink flowers in looser panicles on 55cm (22in) high stems.

Heuchera micrantha Emperor's Cloak in the University of British Columbia Botanical Garden

Forms of **H. grossulariifolia** that are larger than the reduced alpine ones are pretty and graceful. The wild forms that we have seen in unreachable sites had white flowers on reddish 40cm (16in) long stems, and are worth seeking out. Larger forms of **H. cylindrica** are less attractive but interesting; they have stems often to 80cm (31in) high and dingy greenish to creamy white flowers.

H. micrantha does well in a rock garden setting where the climate suits it (e.g. the Pacific coast of North America or northern Europe). The wild form is very pretty growing in moist cliff crevices, as we once saw it on Mary's Peak in western Oregon. It has tiny green-white to pinkish flowers in airy sprays to about 50cm (20in) high. '**Martha Roderick**' is a selection from the wild and has light pink

flowers. '**Painted Lady**' has purple and silver-grey tones in the foliage. There are ruffled leaf forms like '**Ruffles**', '**Ridges**' and '**Krinkles**' from Terra Nova. A seed strain, **Emperor's Cloak**, seems to be a small ruffled form of *H. micrantha* and produces about 50 per cent bronze-foliaged plants.

H. pilosissima is from the coast of California and has fuzzy foliage and small, round, pinkish flowers to about 50cm (20in) high. It was not hardy for us in Pennsylvania but should succeed in warm, dry climates.

H. pubescens is a horticulturally little-known plant from rocky sites in the Appalachians, from Pennsylvania to North Carolina. It is not familiar even in botanic gardens, though it can be abundant in parts of southern Pennsylvania and eastern West

Virginia. It is a very opportunistic grower, being found on rocky slopes in forests, on shaly cliffs and banks, and on rocks. Plants in deep shade and poor soil may consist of a few small leaves and a short stem of flowers, while those perched on rocks in the light will make thick clumps with numerous inflorescences to about 60cm (24in) tall. At Greenland Gap, near Moorefield, West Virginia, where conditions are favourable, *H. pubescens* is conspicuous and handsome on the tumbled sandstone blocks along the road. Plants often have some silver patterning on the leaves. In Hampshire County, West Virginia, we found a population that contains some individuals with foliage that is totally silvery white above.

Many plants grown from this seed are similar and very unusual-looking.

The flowers of *H. pubescens* are large, tubby bells of a luminous pale green, sometimes with reddish petals, and up to 10mm (0.4in) long. They are zygomorphic, with the inner side of the calyx shorter than the outer. Since the bells hang down at an angle, the zygomorphic shape makes the end of the bell level, presumably for the convenience of bees landing and hanging upside down. '**Hob**' is apparently a good winter foliage selection of *H. pubescens* introduced in the UK, but we have not seen it. **_H. alba_** is somewhat similar and has been included in *H. pubescens* by some authorities, although currently it is accepted as a separate

Heuchera maxima at the Rancho Santa Ana Botanic Garden, California

species (PLANTS Database). This occurs in a small geographic area above about 1200m (3950ft) in pockets of peaty, acid soil in fell fields (i.e. expanses of loose rocks) of Oriskany Sandstone in the mountains of West Virginia and Virginia. *H. alba* is a showier plant than *H. pubescens*, with larger, more numerous creamy white flowers in a wider panicle to about the same height. Both of these are very cold-hardy.

H. longiflora is a distinctive species found on moist limestone ledges from southern West Virginia to North Carolina. This is about the same size as *H. pubescens*, and has foliage that is often well mottled with silver and relatively large, to 13.6mm (0.53in) long whitish, tubular flowers held horizontally outward. This sort of flower presentation is usually an adaptation to moth or hummingbird pollination, and is different from the pollination strategies of the other eastern species. *H. longiflora* is rare in nature and unknown in gardens, and we have not yet been able to see it growing or obtain stock.

H. americana var. *hispida*, sometimes considered *H. hispida*, occurs in the same sort of habitats as *H. longiflora*, often clinging to small cracks in wet, limy shale cliffs. It has attractive, rounded leaves, sometimes with large silver patches and contrasting reddish petioles. The purple-tinged flowers are a little larger than those of *H. americana* var. *americana*, being on shorter, 40–60cm (16–24in) long stems.

The montane *H. sanguinea* var. *pulchra* from Arizona has been hardy for us in western Pennsylvania. Our plants are larger than we expected, and have hairy foliage and relatively tight panicles of dark pink flowers about 9mm (0.35in) long of the characteristic trumpet shape (i.e. a tube flared at the end) on 75cm (30in) long stems. There are reportedly forms with silver and dark leaf patterning that would be worth trying if they can be obtained.

Heucheras for naturalizing

A few of the larger heucheras are suitable for naturalizing and will spread slowly by self-

Heuchera americana var. *hispida* in southern West Virginia

seeding. Most of the eastern species can be obtained from nurseries specializing in natives in North America, or from specialist nurseries in the UK.

The wild *H. americana*, exclusive of var. *hispida*, occurs in a variety of sites in eastern North America, from deep woods to crevices in rocks, but it is at its best in light shade on moist banks where it makes tufts of slightly hairy foliage to about 25cm (10in) across. In May and June it sends up tall – to 90cm (3ft) high – naked stems topped with tiny green flowers. In western Pennsylvania the foliage is usually plain green, sometimes with some silvery patterning, but in the southern Appalachians it may be vividly patterned with silver, blue-green and maroon.

All the named selections have been made on the basis of leaf colour; some are a normal part of the variation that will be found in a large group of seedlings. The best of the selections are very beautiful plants. 'Garnet'* retains its heavy maroon spring colour into summer; **Dale's Strain*** has an extreme expression of silver patterning; '**Eco-magnififolia**'* and '**Green Spice**'* have

maroon and silver with a hint of blue. '**Beauty Colour**' (also sold as 'Beauty of Colour') is similar to, but less colourful than, the last two; the name may be less awkward in Dutch.

H. maxima is native to the Santa Barbara Channel Islands and nearby coastal areas of California. The plain green, slightly hairy leaves are about 10–15cm (4–5½in) across, and there are long panicles of small, greenish-white flowers to 60cm (24in) high or more. Because it is from a mild climate, *H. maxima* is reportedly hardy only to about -10°C (14°F), but it is very drought-tolerant and adapted to the rainless summers of southern California, where it can be grown without watering. It has passed this drought resistance to its descendants, the Rancho Santa Ana hybrids (page 29). *H. maxima* resembles *H. villosa* in general aspect, and can be grown in a similar setting. There are plantings under native oaks at the Rancho Santa Ana Botanic Garden in Claremont, California, and it should be suitable for other parts of the world with a Mediterranean climate.

H. villosa is a large species of cliffs and ledges from the Appalachians west to the Ozarks in Arkansas. In the Appalachians *H. villosa* is found to an altitude of at least 1920m (6300ft). The leaves are up to 20cm (8in) across and maple-shaped, with fuzzy petioles. There are 70cm long (27in) wands of tiny whitish flowers during summer. '**Autumn Bride**' has the same green foliage as the wild type but flowers in late summer. **Form *purpurea***, with variably bronzy leaves, occurs occasionally as a wild plant, and selections have been made of it. '**Palace Purple**' was selected in England from a seed lot from North America but degenerated into a mediocre seed strain, and had its Award of Garden Merit from the Royal Horticultural Society rescinded. However, it is still popular and is widely used by out-of-date landscape designers.

Left *Heuchera americana* in western Pennsylvania
Below *Heuchera villosa* f. *purpurea* 'Palace Purple' (an excellent form)

Other bronze selections hold their colour much better over the duration of the season. They include 'Molly Bush'*, hailing originally from Holbrook Nursery, the best dark and purplish form which derives from 'Palace Purple'; 'Bressingham Bronze' which is smaller and has a crisp feel to the foliage, though we haven't found it very vigorous; 'Bronze Wave'*, from The Primrose Path, which is a large, vigorous form with slightly ruffled leaves, and was bred from different f. *purpurea* stock with larger, hairier leaves than 'Palace Purple'.

A type of f. *purpurea* lacking the hairiness of 'Palace Purple' and its close relatives was distributed by We-Du Nurseries of western North Carolina in the 1980s and 1990s as 'We-Du Special'. This has good purple coloration, and has persisted without care in our woodland garden for the last 20 years. It was collected in the Nantahala Gorge in the mountains of western North Carolina, and is probably no longer for sale, but must be extant in quite a number of American gardens.

H. richardsonii is a native of the prairies from the Midwest of North America, into the plains and north well into Canada. It grows among grasses and deep-rooted perennials, with which it must compete for *lebensraum* and water. Plants that we saw in nature at the Fernwood prairie near Niles, Michigan, were relatively small and slender, but when given garden conditions, *H. richardsonii* will become statuesque, making a clump of hairy foliage 50cm (20in) wide and 30cm (12in) tall, with 1m (3½ft) high stems topped with small, greenish flowers.

Heucheras for the perennial bed

Most of the garden heuchera cultivars fall into this category. The only species selections used are those of large forms of **H. cylindrica**. 'Greenfinch', which was introduced by Blooms in 1950, is the best known of these. It has chartreuse flowers on 70cm (28in) stems and silver-patterned foliage.

Hybrid cultivars with green foliage

The **Brizoides group** accounts for the great majority of the garden hybrids that were introduced in the first 80 years of the 20th century. (We use the term Brizoides to refer to this general group rather than to a specific hybrid cross or cultivar.)

The first of them were bred by Lemoine in France before the First World War, and then by Blooms in England from the 1930s up to the present. At least 100 cultivars were given names and marketed, but at this point probably only about 25 are readily available in the UK. In North America there may be as many, but perhaps half of these are plants selected in the USA and apparently are not sold elsewhere. The new fancy foliage hybrids did not push the Brizoides group out of the market, and *The RHS Plant Finder* for 1994–1995 lists about the same number and almost the same selection as the 2004–2005 edition. Apparently this is the number and selection that fits the demands of the gardening public in the UK.

An indication of the importance of the Brizoides group in the minds of those marketing heuchera today is evident in the 104 heuchera photos in the recent Heims and Ware book, only one of which is a traditional Brizoides variety even though they make up about a quarter of the total list of cultivars. With a relatively narrow set of traits to consider (flower colour and size, inflorescence height, and the amount of silvery leaf patterning) why were so many cultivars named and introduced? Breeders following a planned programme naturally wanted to introduce cultivars similar to, but better than their older forms, which would then be dropped. But probably a large number of the introductions were simply due to competition among nurseries who wanted to have their own cultivars, and to satisfy the public's desire for new plants.

In today's market some of the selection names refer to seed strains, either mixed colours, as in the Bressingham hybrids, or single colours, usually bright red, as in Sioux Falls. In the garden centres we have visited in North America most of the Brizoides plants

Heuchera 'Chatterbox' in a Pennsylvania garden

are from these seed strains, which are of course the most economical to propagate. These seed-grown plants are very good, though not as spectacular as some of the Blooms selections, especially those named after members of the family! According to Gary Doerr, head of Blooms North America, the sales of green-leafed Blooms heuchera cultivars over here are so low as to be almost non-existent. That's one reason why we have not made any attempt to grow or see a large sampling of Brizoides, and will mention only a few of those of which we have some personal knowledge. They all have flowers that are either in the shape of an old-fashioned Edison phonograph trumpet (a flared funnel), similar to those of *H. sanguinea*, or are straight-sided bells on stems 40–60cm (16–14in) tall. These plants are usually available from nurseries with general border perennials.

White flowers: '**June Bride**' did well for us, and has creamy white flowers. **White Cloud*** is a good seed strain and has nice silvering on the leaves.

Pink flowers: our favourite is '**Rosemary Bloom**'* which has large, pure pink flowers of the *sanguinea* form. '**Chatterbox**', '**Patricia**

Louise', and '**Pretty Polly**' are vigorous pinks available in North America. '**Brandon Pink**' is a very hardy selection from Manitoba.

Red flowers: '**Firebird**'* is the most impressive red-flowering Brizoides cultivar we have seen. '**Mt. St. Helens**' is a Sunny Border introduction. '**Northern Fire**' is another very hardy selection from Manitoba. Other red types, e.g. **Firefly**, **Frackel** and **Sioux Falls**, have become seed strains. We have an excellent plant that we bought wrongly labelled that has large, dark red flowers on 60cm (24in) high stems. This seems to be the new '**Ruby Bells**'.

Another small group of plants are related to *H.* 'Chiqui' and *H.* 'Coral Bouquet', i.e. hybrids between *H. brizoides* and *H. cylindrica*, but are larger, since the *H. cylindrica* parent was of the tall form rather than the short var. *alpina*. '**Raspberry Regal**', introduced in 1985, has dull, reddish flowers with a green tinge: '**Florist's Choice**' (Terra Nova, 2000) has a clearer red flower colour. Both of these have cattail-shaped inflorescences to about 75cm (30in).

Other green-leafed hybrid cultivars include the **Rancho Santa Ana hybrids**. These *H. maxima* x *H. sanguinea* hybrids from the

Rancho Santa Ana Botanic Garden, California, make an effect similar to the Brizoides types, although the inflorescences are larger and more open and airy because of the input of the *H. maxima* parent (see page 120 for notes on breeding these hybrids). Because of their drought resistance they should be useful in dry-climate gardening where winter temperatures do not go lower than about –10°C (14°F). We have not seen any evidence that they are used in Europe, but they should do well in mild-climate areas. They are all relatively large, with leaves 7–8cm (2¾–3½in) across and flowers to about 60cm (24in) high. '**Opal**' has somewhat globular white flowers from pink buds, '**Wendy**'* and '**Genevieve**' have pink flowers, '**Susanna**' has near-red dark pink flowers, and '**Santa Ana Cardinal**'* is bright red. '**Old La Rochette**' was produced by another breeder, Victor Reiter, and is not properly a Santa Ana hybrid but has the same parentage. This is another pink-flowered cultivar. '**Lillian's Pink**' is an *H. pilosissima* x *H. sanguinea* hybrid and has nearly globular pink flowers on 50cm (20in)

high stems, and was introduced by the California Flora Nursery.

The **Larenim hybrids** are a set of plants introduced by The Primrose Path in the late 1980s. They were a result of crosses between an especially good pink-flowered Brizoides, grown from the seed of Bressingham hybrids, and *H. pubescens* grown from seed from Larenim Park in Mineral County, West Virginia. The Larenims have green foliage, and pink or pink and white funnel-shaped flowers 7–9mm (0.3–0.35in) long on stems to 45–60cm (18–24in) high.

'**Larenim Queen**' is a selection of one of these hybrids and has lightly silver-marbled green foliage and pink flowers to 60cm (24in) high. '**Winter Red**' was chosen on the basis of its outstanding red foliage during the winter, and has pink flowers to 50cm (20in) high. '**White Marble**', the first heuchera hybrid produced at The Primrose Path, is not a Larenim hybrid but has similar parentage (*H. pubescens* x Brizoides White Cloud). This is a large vigorous heuchera with thick crowns and deep roots, green foliage marbled with

Heuchera 'Lillian's Pink' at the Rancho Santa Ana Botanic Garden, California

Heuchera Larenim hybrid

silver, and flower stems to 75cm (30in). The flowers are about 8mm (0.3in) long and white, aging to pinkish, and have relatively large petals that have caused some distributors to refer to them as 'double'. The last two cultivars are available at a few specialist nurseries.

Early on, between 1993 and 1996, Terra Nova offered a few ruffled hybrids with green leaves, in addition to the ruffled forms of *H. micrantha* mentioned above. The most popular hybrid was '**Strawberry Swirl**', a cross between *H. micrantha* 'Ruffles' and an *H. sanguinea* selection. This vigorous plant has ruffled, silvered green leaves, and small

teardrop pink flowers to about 50cm (20in) high, but it was not reliably winter-hardy for us. It is still widely available.

Hybrid cultivars with bronze foliage

The term 'bronze' covers everything from tan to dark red-purple, and breeders put great value on the ability of plants to hold the reddish-purple new foliage colour through the season without 'greening out'. Environmental factors such as temperature, light intensity and soil moisture affect the foliage colour, and some cultivars look quite different from one garden to another, and from one month to another, making plant recognition quite a difficult task.

Mary Ramsdale in England made a short series of hybrids between *H. villosa* 'Palace Purple' and Brizoides. Several of these, including '**David**', which resembles 'Palace Purple' with larger white flowers, and '**Rachel**', which has light bronze leaves and small pink flowers, were introduced in the early 1990s. Only 'Rachel' seems to be available at this time.

Montrose Ruby*, the original cross made at Montrose Nursery in the 1980s between *H.*

villosa 'Palace Purple' and *H. americana* Dale's Strain, has largely been eclipsed by newer bronze and silver forms, but in good forms it is still one of the best of the foliage-only bronze heucheras. Our clone has the vigour of *H. villosa* 'Bronze Wave', and it can be used in naturalizing, as a landscape plant and in the border. The leaves have silver markings on a rich purple background, and tiny white flowers in early summer.

Primrose Path bronze hybrids: '**Tinian Bronze**' is the earliest of the bronze cultivars

Heuchera 'Rachel'

from The Primrose Path. This was a remake of the cross that resulted in Montrose Ruby and involved *H. villosa* f. *purpurea* of the We-Du Special type x *H. americana* Dale's Strain. 'Tinian Bronze' has dark purple-bronze leaves about 10–12cm (4–4½in) across, with bluish markings on the veins above and tiny greenish flowers. It is probably not available from nurseries now. **'Quilters' Joy'*** was named because the silver and bronze leaf surface resembles appliqué patchwork. This still compares well with newer forms and has angular leaves about 8cm (3½in) across, and upright, medium-sized off-white flowers to 60cm (24in) high. This is often incorrectly sold as **'Checkers'**.

'**Regina'*** has larger, rounded, silvered leaves and medium-sized light pink flowers to 60cm (24in). 'Harmonic Convergence' has fairly similar foliage, but differs in that it has conical inflorescences of larger, frilly, light pink flowers to about 50cm (20in) high. '**Rose Mirrors**' has medium pink flowers about 6mm (0.2in) long on 50cm (20in) high stems, and dark purple leaves with central silvering. '**Rose Majesty**' is larger, with 7mm (0.3in) medium pink flowers on 60cm (24in) stems, and lighter bronze and silver foliage. '**Midnight Burgundy**' is a compact plant with very dark, almost slate grey and silver foliage, and small cream flowers to 45cm (18in) high. '**Petite Marbled Burgundy'*** (previously mentioned with the other Petites as a rock garden plant) will become considerably larger when given rich soil, making thick clumps of bronze and silver leaves 6cm (2½in) wide, and erect stems of medium-sized light pink flowers to 45cm (18in) high.

In the Silver Series, introduced from the late 1990s, there is '**Silver Scrolls'*** with rounded, almost totally metallic silver leaves 8cm (3½in) across, marked with a scrollwork of dark veining and narrow panicles of small white flowers from pink buds on 70cm (27in) long stems. '**Silver Lode**' has similar, though matt, silvered leaves and greenish-white flowers. '**Silver Maps**' is smaller, but there's less contrast in the metallic silvered leaves,

though there are larger white flowers to 50cm (20in) high. '**Raspberry Ice'*** has more angular bronze and metallic silver leaves, and medium-sized pink flowers to 50cm (20in) high. And '**Silver Light**' is a small form with almost totally metallic silver leaves 6cm (2½in) across and light pink flowers to 40cm (16in) high. '**Jade Gloss**' also belongs in this group, and has matt silver leaves with wide vein markings in bronze; the leaves tend to curl up slightly at the edges, showing off the red-purple undersides. The medium-sized white flowers are on 45cm (18in) long stems. Among the newer introductions are '**Royal Velvet**' with dark purple and silver fuzzy foliage, and medium white flowers to 50cm (20in) high, '**Hearts on Fire**' with ruffled red and silver leaves in especially thick clumps and small white flowers, also to 50cm (20in), and '**Shenandoah Mountain**', a very large form with soft bronze and silver foliage in a clump up to 50cm (20in) across, and many leafy stems with medium-sized creamy flowers to 90cm (3ft) high.

The most recent set of hybrids have erect stems of large flowers, and are the result of new crosses using *H. alba*. Those just released are '**Purple Mountain Majesty**' with purple foliage lightly marked with silver, and almost globular creamy white flowers about 9mm (0.35in) long on 50cm (20in) long stems, and '**Moonlight'*** with chequered purple and silver foliage, and large pale green flowers on dark purple stems of about the same length. A very different looking plant is '**Frosted Violet'*** (sold in Europe as '**Frosted Violet Dream**'), which resembles *H. villosa* f. *purpurea*, which is one parent, though with pink-violet suffused silvering on the leaves. This makes clumps about 40cm (16in) across and 25cm (10in) high with 8cm (3½in) wide leaves and 60cm (24in) high wands of small, pink flowers in early summer.

Terra Nova bronze hybrids: A long series of cultivars was bred from Montrose Ruby and *H. americana* by Terra Nova and introduced in the 1990s. These are all variations on the basic theme of bronze leaves with a silvery pattern,

as described, and differ in the tone of the bronze, the extent of silver, crispness of markings, glossiness, and so on. The hybrids include '**Pewter Veil**', '**Amethyst Myst**', '**Burgundy Frost**', '**Cascade Dawn**', '**Cathedral Windows**', '**Persian Carpet**', '**Plum Pudding**'*, '**Purple Sails**', '**Regal Robe**', '**Ruby Veil**', '**Silver Shadows**' and '**Velvet Night**'. Their tiny, greenish flowers are on long stems, and most are fairly similar to each other; they can hardly be distinguished at times in summer, and many have since dropped out of the market.

'**Ebony and Ivory**' is distinctive, with small white flowers and contrasting dark bronze and silver foliage. It is very handsome in the Pacific Northwest and north-western Europe, but does not seem to perform very well in eastern North America. '**Sparkling Burgundy**' and '**Starry Night**' are new cultivars with medium-sized white flowers to about 50cm (20in) high over red-bronze foliage. '**Vesuvius**' has pink flowers on 40cm (16in) long stems over light bronze foliage. The new '**Obsidian**'* has very dark bronze foliage with no silver, purple in the spring and darkest green in summer. '**Smokey Rose**' has small pale pink flowers and light bronze leaves.

Terra Nova also produced a series of bronze hybrids that have ruffled foliage acquired from *H. micrantha* 'Ruffles'. '**Purple Petticoats**'* has been the best ruffled heuchera for us, retaining its colour well and surviving our winters without damage. '**Stormy Seas**' is a large, vigorous form, though '**Can Can**' is smaller and less vigorous. Both forms have silver patterning, but 'green out' during the season. The non-silver '**Ruby Ruffles**' and '**Chocolate Ruffles**' also turn green, but apparently are borderline hardy in cold climates. All these ruffled forms have insignificant flowers. More recent ruffled cultivars have light bronze foliage and, in the case of '**Fireworks**', small light pink flowers, while '**Cherries Jubilee**' is light red (both are relatively compact).

Left *Heuchera* 'Purple Mountain Majesty'
Right *Heuchera* 'Pewter Veil'

Other bronze hybrids have been introduced, especially by plantsmen in the Netherlands. '**Pewter Moon**', which comes from Piet Oudolf, has rounded, slightly cupped leaves that resemble one of the Silver Series from The Primrose Path, and small white flowers on 40cm (16in) long stems, though it has not been vigorous with us. '**Silver Indiana**', from van den Top, has rounded, highly silvered leaves and small white flowers to about 40cm (16in). '**Blackbird**', coming from Aart Wijnhout, has purple leaves and small pink flowers to 45cm (18in). '**Swirling Fantasy**', also from Wijnhout, is similar in foliage and habit to 'Regina', of which it is a seedling, and has darker pink flowers (not red as advertised). '**Crimson Curls**', a very ruffled form grown in England from the seed of 'Chocolate Ruffles', is a highly promoted new plant. Many more cultivars, mostly derived from seed from American breeders' plants, are coming from the Netherlands.

Heuchera 'Ruby Ruffles' at the Center for Conservation Education, Westmoreland County, Pennsylvania

Heuchera 'Crimson Curls' at the Center for Conservation Education, Westmoreland County, Pennsylvania

Sports (Mutations)

What are gardeners supposed to do with them? Because they are rare, nurserymen assume that they are desirable and introduce them with thoughts of early retirement. But, in the case of heucheras, they are the walking wounded and will soon die a pathetic death without the sort of pampering that got them to the sale bench in the garden centre. Gardeners usually use them singly as 'accents', which means that they don't fit into their design scheme, and grow them just because they are rare and odd, and their friends don't have them. We admit that we have tried some of these, but have none left at present. We also admit that we have a variegated sport of *H.* 'Regina' that we just might introduce.

Heuchera sports seen in nurseries generally fall into two categories. The first has the familiar variegated foliage. These forms have patches of differently coloured tissue in the leaves where the normal pigment, usually chlorophyll, has not been made by the plant. Because of the way the tissues form in the leaf buds, variegation in monocots, such as sedges and hostas, appears as white or yellow stripes on the leaf surface. In dicots, such as heucheras and maple trees, the variegation occurs as light coloured patches and streaks or stippling. In green-leafed plants the patches are white or yellowish, but in purple-leafed plants the subtraction of green pigment leaves dark pink patches. Variegated forms like this generally do not breed true, so each plant is an isolated find. Plants of the second type are lacking the genes controlling the ability to make a pigment, so that the whole plant is yellow or very pale green. This sort of sport can produce similar seedlings. Not commonly seen in heucheras in the commercial market are mutations that affect the growth form, and produce grotesquely shaped growth, cupped leaves, or distorted flowers.

Variegated *Heuchera americana* from wild seed from northern West Virginia

A number of white-variegated sports of Brizoides heuchera have been put on the market by Terra Nova. They include '**Coral Splash**', '**Frosty**', '**Monet**', '**Snow Storm**' and '**Splish Splash**' and have pink to red flowers, as does '**Gold Dust**', with light yellow variegation. '**Hailstorm**', with white variegation and red flowers, comes from Monksilver Nursery in England. '**Snow Angel**', from Bluebird Nursery in Nebraska, has white variegation and pink flowers, and seems to be the most enduring and popular form in North America.

There are also variegated forms of bronze cultivars. They are more curious than attractive, and are often picked out of tissue culture where they occur fairly commonly (page 146), and are grown on to see if they are viable. '**Mardi Gras**' with purple spots on an orange-pink background, and '**Peachy Keen**' with pink-red leaves blotched purple, are Terra Nova's contributions to this set.

Belonging to the second type of colour sport are a number of recently introduced heucheras. They, too, occur regularly in tissue culture and can be carefully isolated and grown on for evaluation. '**Amber Waves**', a colour sport of a ruffled, bronze foliage form, has leaves that are yellow-tan above and purple below. This has been very slow-growing for nurserymen. Apparently it isn't very hardy, although we have not had a chance to test it since our plant did not survive the summer. '**Marmalade**' has yellow-bronze foliage and is supposedly more vigorous. '**Lime Rickey**' and the very similar '**Key Lime Pie**' are sickly yellow green forms (all are Terra Nova introductions). 'Key Lime Pie' is one of a set named for desserts that is being marketed by Proven Winners.

Heuchera 'Caramel' (photo by Regina Birchem)

The 2005 French introduction '**Caramel**' apparently is a sport of the bronze *H. villosa*, and though we have not yet seen it, Dutch nurserymen seem to be very excited about it. It has waved leaves 15cm (6in) across, shaped like those of *H. villosa*, and is orange to pale yellow above and red-purple below. It should have more vigour than the other yellow forms.

In the bizarre growth category from Terra Nova we do have, though, '**Peacock Feathers**', a tissue culture sport of 'Plum Pudding' with 3.5cm (1½in) long feather-shaped leaves. Similar tissue culture sports of various cultivars arise occasionally in our cultures at The Primrose Path. They are not generally vigorous enough to survive in the garden.

HEUCHERELLA – FOAMY BELLS

The common name – foamy bells – is a recent one that we think was coined by Tony Avent of Plant Delights Nursery. It is an apt term that has come into general use.

The heucherellas now on the market are a diverse group, having been derived from separate crosses between *Heuchera* and *Tiarella*, and these genera have undergone a great proliferation of forms since the late 1980s. The heuchera parents used in the crosses have all been from the group that we considered as heucheras for the perennial bed. The heucherellas available have the same general cultivation requirements, which are also those that suit tiarellas. Furthermore, the sizes of mature clumps are similar to those of tiarellas. The problem has been that heucherellas differ widely in their vigour when grown under open garden conditions. Plants that thrive in pots or in a special bed that is kept moist and heavily fertilized may fade away under conditions of stress from competition, and less than ideal weather conditions.

The foliage of heucherellas combines the traits of the parent types to make novel, and often very beautiful, effects. As with the parents, the dark markings on the leaf surface depend greatly on environmental factors, and new spring growth will have much heavier markings than mature foliage. Note, though, that the bronze forms tend to 'green out' over summer. The flowers are intermediate in size and shape to their parents', so their showiness depends largely on having heuchera parents with good flowers. In forms with good flowers, the flower colour is usually white or with a pink calyx and white petals. From a normal viewing distance the latter give a pink impression, and will be referred to as pink.

Green foliage heucherellas

These include the earliest of the heucherellas to be introduced, and are plants with a Brizoides heuchera as one parent. *H. tiarelloides*, or perhaps more correctly 'Tiarelloides', is a running plant with pink flowers; *H. tiarelloides* 'Alba' is clumping and has white flowers. They are Lemoine plants that we have never seen for sale or even grown in North America, though the former is apparently available in the UK. '**Bridget Bloom**', from Blooms of Bressingham, has leaves lightly marked with maroon and pink flowers on 40cm (16in) long stems.

'**Rosalie**' has the interior of the leaf heavily marked with maroon, and small pink flowers to about 30cm (12in). '**Pink Frost**', '**Snow White**' and '**White Blush**' are all siblings from The Primrose Path and have leaves lightly marked with maroon and silver, and medium pink, white, and pale pink flowers, respectively, on stems to 50cm (20in) long. '**Checkered White**' was a large form with silver and dark green foliage, and white flowers but may no longer be available. '**Heart of Darkness**'* is a recent introduction from The Primrose Path, and has leaves with a maroon centre surrounded by silver and by green; the abundant white flowers grow to 60cm (24in) high.

Terra Nova has introduced the following: '**Cranberry Ice**', which has green leaves with maroon centres and pink flowers; the pink-flowering '**Crimson Clouds**' with leaves marked with maroon and unusual doubled veining; '**Dayglow Pink**', with deeply lobed, maroon marked leaves and small pink flowers (and which is very tiarella-like); '**Party Time**', with deeply lobed leaves marked with maroon and silver, and light pink flowers; '**Viking Ship**' with deeply lobed silvered leaves and pink flowers; and, best of all, '**Kimono**'*, with green, maroon, and silver leaves deeply lobed and the middle lobe extended, though unfortunately the flowers are poor yellow-green. '**Pink Gem**', which is being marketed by Proven Winners, has similar leaves, and pink flowers.

Heucherella 'Checkered White'

Bronze foliage heucherellas

'**Quicksilver**'*, from The Primrose Path, has leaves surfaced with metallic silver, and light pink flowers from medium pink buds on 50cm (20in) long stems. '**Cinnamon Bear**' has indistinctly marked, deeply lobed leaves, and yellowish-green flowers. '**Silver Streak**' has deeply lobed and silvered leaves, and scanty white flowers to about 30cm (12in) high. '**Burnished Bronze**'* has deeply cut, evenly coloured chocolate bronze leaves with faint central darker maroon markings, and light pink flowers to about 35cm (14in). It has been an especially enduring form in our garden. The recently introduced '**Chocolate Lace**' seems hardly distinguishable. '**Birthday Cake**' has deeply lobed dark bronze foliage and white flowers. The last five are from Terra Nova.

Heucherella sports

'**Sunspot**' is a selection of a tissue culture sport of 'Dayglow Pink' that lost its chlorophyll and came out with yellow foliage with a central blotch which is more red than maroon.

Heucherella 'Dayglow Pink'

Tiarella cordifolia 'Running Tapestry'

'**Stoplight**' is a hybrid involving a yellow foliage heuchera as a parent. It has white flowers and larger leaves marked in a more reddish way than 'Sunspot. Both are from Terra Nova. '**Gold**', from Proven Winners, has yellow, deeply lobed leaves with maroon along the main veins and pink flowers, and seems generally similar to 'Sunspot'.

TIARELLA – FOAM FLOWERS

The current nomenclature of this group by botanical authorities differs considerably from traditional horticultural usage. Currently just three species are recognized: *T. cordifolia* in eastern North America, *T. trifoliata* in western North America, and *T. polyphylla* in east Asia. These are plants for the woodland garden or, in the case of the showier new hybrids, a more formal shaded bed. Like heucheras, tiarellas change in appearance through the year. The spring foliage is often attractively flushed with red-bronze, though the maroon markings on the leaves fade as the weather warms in summer, but increase in intensity as autumn approaches. The autumn foliage may turn dark red with the onset of cool temperatures.

Tiarella 'Braveheart'

Species selections

T. cordifolia is divided into *T. cordifolia* **var. cordifolia** and *T. c.* **var. australis**, which are stoloniferous forms, and *T. c.* **var. collina**, which is a clumping form from south-eastern North America. A number of wild selections have been made of *T. c.* var. *cordifolia* and introduced for garden use; all have white flowers to about 35cm (14in) high. '**Brandywine**' is a form with light maroon markings on the leaves. '**Running Tapestry**'* has rounded leaves with heavy maroon markings. '**Slick Rock**' has small plain green, rather pointed leaves and skimpy flowers and runs quickly. '**Laird of Skye**' resembles a larger form of 'Slick Rock'. '**Glossy**' has especially shiny leaves and white flowers. And '**Eco Red Heart**' has leaves marked with a central maroon blotch.

Within *T. c.* var. *collina*, *T. wherryi*, sometimes considered a separate species, is a class of plants that has matt, light green foliage. *T.* **var. excelsa** seems to be a form name for plants with deeply lobed leaves. '**Montrose Selection**'* is an especially vividly coloured selection of var. *collina* introduced by Montrose Nursery in North Carolina in the late 1980s. It has dark green leaves, dark stems and pink flowers. '**Oakleaf**' and '**Dunvegan**' are selections with deeply lobed leaves and pink flowers from Dunvegan Nursery in eastern Pennsylvania. '**George Shenk Pink**' is a *wherryi* type that flowers with pink flowers about two weeks later than most others. '**Bronze Beauty**' has bronzed, deeply lobed spring foliage and pink flowers. '**Braveheart**' has deeply lobed leaves with a large central maroon patch, and pink flowers. And '**Spring Bronze**' has dark red-bronze spring foliage and pink flowers. The last two are from The Primrose Path. '**Skid's Variegated**', an English variety, and '**Heronswood Mist**', from Heronswood Nursery in Washington State, both have leaves freckled with white variegation and white flowers. All make thick clumps with erect stems of flowers to 35–40cm (14–16in) long in fuller panicles than those of *T. c.* var. *cordifolia*.

T. trifoliata **var.** *trifoliata*, with lobed to compound leaves, its form *laciniata* with compound and finely cut leaves, and the larger *T. trifoliata* **var.** *unifoliata* with rounded entire leaves, all have plain green foliage and white flowers in sparse panicles on spreading stems to about 45cm (18in) high. No named selections seem to have been made of them. *T. polyphylla* from east Asia has rounded cordate leaves, and thin panicles of small white or pink flowers to about 35cm (14in). This has not been hardy for us, and is grown much more commonly in Europe than in North America. The names '**Moorgrun**' and '**Filigran**' are used as cultivar names, but are apparently seed strains and do not seem to differ from the usual seed-grown plants under the species name. '*Baoxing Pink*', from Crug Nursery in Wales, and '*Balang Pink*', listed by Long Acre Plants in England, are selections with especially good pink flowers.

Tiarella trifoliata in the University of British Columbia Botanical Garden

Tiarella 'Tiger Stripe' in winter

Hybrid tiarellas

The breeding programmes of The Primrose Path and Terra Nova Nurseries have produced parallel arrays of complex tiarella hybrids. We will discuss the history of this in detail in Chapter 5.

Primrose Path hybrids

'**Tiger Stripe**' is a vigorous hybrid involving several of the eastern forms. This has cordate leaves with seasonally variable maroon striping and pink flowers to about 40cm (18in). The **Trifoliate hybrids** were a group of plants from crosses between 'Tiger Stripe' and *T. trifoliata* var. *trifoliata* f. *laciniata* that were introduced at the beginning of the 1990s. '**Filigree Lace**', a plant selected from this group of hybrids, is still occasionally offered by nurseries. It has cut leaves and white flowers in loose panicles.

The back-crosses of these hybrids to 'Tiger Stripe' have inflorescences increasingly resembling those of 'Tiger Stripe', while retaining the lacy foliage of form *laciniata*: '**Martha Oliver**'* has deeply cut, maroon-marked leaves and white flowers; '**Elizabeth Oliver**'* has fragrant light pink flowers and heavily maroon-marked cut foliage. Crosses among the best forms of this type have given new hybrids with exaggerated traits from both sides of the original hybrids: '**Arpeggio**' has maroon-marked, fingered leaves and white flowers; '**Green Sword**'* has deeply lobed leaves with the central lobe much elongated and white flowers; '**Butterfly Wings**' has lacy, maroon-marked compound leaves with the segments held on two planes, and white flowers; '**Pink Brushes**'* is a large and vigorous form with deeply lobed maroon-marked leaves, and dense pink flower spikes over an extended time. All the foregoing are clump-formers, but **'Lace Carpet'**, a cross between 'Elizabeth Oliver' and 'Slick Rock' is a small, white-flowered runner with very cut foliage. **'Running Tiger'*** is a much larger stoloniferous form with deeply lobed leaves, maroon-blotched leaves and white flowers to 40cm (16in). **'Summer Snow'**, with white flowers, and **'Pink Pearls'***, with light pink flowers, are crosses of *T. c.* var. *collina* to *T. t.* var. *unifoliata* and have entire, rounded leaves and flower with 45cm (18in) spreading inflorescences from late May well into summer.

Terra Nova hybrids

Terra Nova's plants have almost all been cultivars with a clumping habit, maroon-marked leaves, and flowers of the *collina* conformation on 30–40cm (12–18in) long stems. There are a few cultivars with entire leaves: **'Inkblot'**, with a dark central blotch and pink flowers, and **'Pirate's Patch'**, with a central blotch and white flowers; **'Lacquer Leaf'**, with unmarked very glossy leaves and white flowers; and **'Dark Eyes'**, a cultivar with pink flowers and a central blotch on the leaves, which makes short stolons.

There is a by now bewilderingly long series of hybrids (some similar in appearance) that differ in details of leaf cutting and shape of leaf segments, and the amount of maroon leaf blotching and flower colour. White-flowered forms include: **'Black Velvet'**, **'Iron Butterfly'**, **'Neon Lights'**, **'Pin Wheel'**, **'Sea Foam'***, **'Skeleton Key'** and **'Starfish.'** Pink flowered forms include: **'Black Snowflake'**, **'Candy Striper'**, **'Crow Feather'**, **'Cygnet'**, **'Mint Chocolate'**, **'Ninja'**, **'Pink Bouquet'** (which is scented), **'Pink Skyrocket'**, **'Spanish Cross'**, **'Spring Symphony'** and **'Sugar and Spice'**. Of all these, we think that 'Sea Foam' has the most strikingly cut and patterned foliage, which is combined with excellent vigour. **'Jeepers Creepers'** is a stoloniferous form with cut, maroon-striped leaves and white flowers. Two additional clumping plants being marketed by Proven Winners are **'Mercury'**, with deeply cut leaves heavily marked with maroon, and

'Venus', with similarly shaped leaves without maroon. Both have pink flowers.

OTHER GENERA

In the other genera that we are considering there has been no breeding work done, and with a couple of exceptions the plants used in the garden are the wild forms.

Mitella

M. diphylla* is a wildflower of eastern North America, and resembles a tiarella with entire, angular, slightly hairy leaves about 6cm (2½in) across; in spring it has tiny white snowflake flowers in narrow spikes to 45cm (18in) high. Plants grown in the woodland garden will make attractive clumps of foliage 25cm (10in) across and 20cm (8in) tall. *M. stylosa** of eastern Asia makes a more compact foliage clump 20cm (8in) across and only 6cm (2½in) high. The leaves are sharply angular and long in proportion, and are mottled with silvery grey-green. There are many stems of small red-purple flowers to 40cm (16in) high.

M. japonica, with plain green leaves, is similar and included in the latter species by some. *M. japonica* **'Variegata'** has the leaves irregularly blotched with white. There are a number of other species that grow as thin clumps of a few leaves, with tiny green flowers on slender stems to about 25cm (10in). *M. nuda* from the northern USA and Canada, and *M. breweri* and *M. caulescens* from the mountains of western North America, are included in this group and are worth growing in a shady wild garden.

Tellima

T. grandiflora, from western North America from Alaska to California, is the only member of the genus and resembles a very large mitella. It has rounded, hairy leaves to 8cm (3½in) across and wands of fringy green to pinkish flowers 40–80cm (16–32in) tall. It is quite drought-tolerant as it can occur in forests

Above *Tellima grandiflora* at the Memorial University Botanical Garden, Newfoundland
Left *Mitella breweri* in the Cascade Mountains, Oregon

where there is little summer rainfall. For fragrant flowers, choose **var. *odorata***. 'Forest Frost' is a selection with the leaves marked with patches of silver. The quality of the markings may depend on climate, because plants that we have had in our garden in Pennsylvania show only faint indications of silver, whereas photos we have taken on our trips to the Pacific Northwest show heavy markings. There are also plants with reddish leaf coloration that develops in late summer and lasts into winter. These plants are referred to as the Rubra Group or, better, as f. *purpurea*. One of these, '**Purpurteppich**' ('Purple Tipped'), has leaves shaded reddish toward the margins, and purple veining. The colour is most intense in late summer. The variegated cultivar '**Delphine**' has pale green foliage marked with cream. The latter cultivars are sold in Europe; we have not seen cultivars other than 'Forest Frost' for sale in North America.

Tiarella 'Pink Skyrockets'

3 Using heucheras and tiarellas in the garden

AESTHETICS AND CULTURAL REQUIREMENTS

Combining plants is both the joy and the despair of gardeners. A gardener can be entirely taken over by a dream of violet and orange flowers and silver foliage, working for years to create such a scheme backed by shrubs, auditioning plants until the results are perfect (except that they never are!). Or perhaps, seized by Gertrude Jekyll's description of her long border at Munstead Wood, the gardener puts together a pink and white mix (certainly easier than violet and orange) with cooling silver leaves, trying to reproduce a small part of her famous scheme. Juggling the flowering period, soil, water and pH requirements, the height and texture, and the rhythm of the plants, and then fine-tuning can keep a gardener happy for years, even decades.

However, a combination which works well one year may fail the next, since plants flower according to their own timetables, and these timetables are activated by different factors. Cool, wet weather, or hot, dry winds, pests and diseases or late frosts can spoil a carefully planned effect. And a scheme of lemon-yellow lilies arranged to contrast with a bright blue anchusa can be ruined overnight by a herd of rampaging deer.

One tactic for overcoming the vagaries of nature is to select plants with a long flowering period, and to cultivate an appreciation for foliage, while trying a large number of individual plants hoping that some, at least, will perform. And that's where heucheras come in. They are especially rewarding as border plants since many of them tolerate a

good deal of sun, and their evergreen, purple foliage is a good addition to many schemes. Also, their pink and white flowers, and maroon and burgundy foliage, are excellent when combined with shrubs of similar hues. As Gertrude Jekyll pointed out, placing similar colours together emphasizes the differences among them. Consequently a scheme of purple-leaf heucheras backed by a weeping purple beech, *Physocarpus* 'Diablo', a maroon weigela such as 'Wine and Roses' and *Prunus cistena* (purple-leafed sand cherry) would stand out in the sun and glow on misty days. Because it depends so heavily on foliage for its effect, it would stand out for six months or longer. Add some burgundy daylilies, pink or white tulips and chrysanthemums, and you extend the season of interest even further. Just be sure that all your selections enjoy similar, well-drained gritty soil that's near neutral, with ample nutrients, and it'll look terrific.

Tiarellas offer extra possibilities since they can thrive even in deep shade, flowering where other plants would not. They need a humus-rich, moist situation, and selecting companions is easy. Any woodlanders that like a neutral pH (ruling out the ericaceous plants such as rhododendrons, azaleas, laurel, heaths, heathers and blueberries) will enjoy this setting. Try weaving together *Phlox stolonifera*, wild gingers, ferns, cimicifugas and *Eupatorium rugosum* in an eastern North American scheme, or combine them very effectively with hostas, epimediums, tricyrtis and ferns in a garden with an east Asian flavour. For more specific ideas relating to both heucheras and tiarellas, using plants with similar cultural requirements, read on.

A maroon and silver shady island bed

A dark leaved redbud, *Cercis canadensis* 'Forest Pansy,' is the centrepiece for this garden. It is surrounded by burgundy and silver leaf heucheras and similar companion plants. A *Prunus cistena*, trained as a tree, would also be appropriate, or *Cotinus coggygria* (purple smoke tree).

1 *Cercis* 'Forest Pansy'
2 *Heuchera* 'Frosted Violet'
3 *Heucherella* 'Quicksilver'
4 *Heuchera* 'Raspberry Ice'
5 *H.* 'Moonlight'
6 *H.* 'Plum Pudding'
7 *H.* 'Obsidian'
8 *H.* 'Purple Petticoats'
9 *H.* 'Silver Scrolls'
10 *Athyrium niponicum* f. *pictum*
11 *Heucherella* 'Kimono'
12 *Pulmonaria* 'Roy Davidson'
13 *Lamium* 'Orchid Frost'
14 *Carex morrowii*
15 *Athyrium* 'Branford Beauty'
16 *Sedum ternatum*

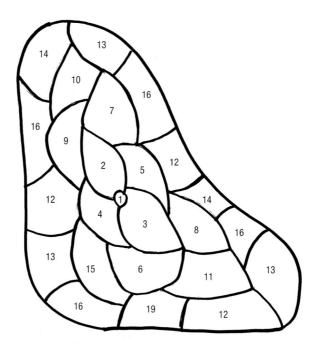

COMBINATIONS USING FOLIAGE COLOURS AS THE THEME

Maroon and burgundy-foliaged plants as companions

Although some of the plants advertised as violet turn out to be a muddy bronze as the season progresses, some retain their dark colour through the season. The best ones are constantly being replaced by even better forms, so check with your local nursery to find the newest cultivars. When seeking specific colour forms for a desired effect, be sure to emphasize this to the nurseryman.

If you've got mature copper beech trees to surround with maroon foliage plants, you are very lucky. Other large trees with the potential to be the centre of such a planting include

Acer 'Crimson King' and *Betula* 'Crimson Frost' (purple birch). Smaller trees to combine with similar foliage are *Acer palmatum* 'Sherwood Flame' or any of the dark red Japanese maples, and also *Cercis canadensis* 'Forest Pansy' (purple redbud) and *Cotinus coggygria* 'Velvet Cloak' (purple smoke bush).

Smaller shrubs suitable for this scheme include many berberis, such as 'Crimson Velvet' or 'Royal Burgundy', *Weigela* 'Alexander' or 'Midnight Wine', and *Physocarpus opulifolius* 'Diablo' (purple ninebark).

Perennials to enhance the scheme include *Ajuga* 'Burgundy Glow', *Foeniculum vulgare* 'Purpurea' (bronze fennel), *Lysimachia ciliata* 'Firecracker' (purple-leafed loosestrife), the purple form of culinary sage (*Salvia officinalis*), and *Sedum* 'Moorchen' and 'Arthur Branch'.

Purple-leaved heuchera and *Cercis* 'Forest Pansy'

Likely annuals include *Perilla frutescens,* giant red Indian mustard, and even 'Purple Ruffles' basil.

But all this purple foliage can be overwhelming and, without any contrast, even boring, which is where the silvery blues come in.

Using silvery-blue foliage plants as companions

Juniperus scopulorum 'Moonglow' and *Cupressus arizonica* 'Blue Ice' would be two top candidates for cooling off maroon and burgundy plants. Or try *Cupressocyparis* x *leylandii* 'Naylor's Blue' or *Salix elaeagnos,* a white leaf willow. *Eleagnus commutata* (silverberry) would be a good choice, or even *Chamaecyparis pisifera* 'Curly Top', a selection of the boulevard cypress. For contrasting winter interest in the stems, add *Cornus alba* 'Ivory Halo' (red osier dogwood), or *Juniperus squamata* 'Blue Star' for all-year silver foliage.

Silvery blue foliaged perennials are easy to find and use, with the ever popular *Stachys byzantia* (lamb's ears) and *Artemesia* 'Silver Mound' (or any of the silver leaf artemesias,

and there's a wide choice) leading the pack. Add silver grasses such as *Festuca* 'Elijah Blue' or *Helioctotrichon sempervirens* (blue oat grass). An eryngium such as 'Miss Willmott's Ghost' adds an interesting texture.

Once you have the background, or 'bones' of the planting, fill in the foreground with the maroon- and burgundy-leafed heucheras, and also other maroon-flowering plants. Try *Salvia verticillata* 'Purple Rain', *S.* 'East Frieslands', *Tradescantia* 'Concord Grape' and *Knautia macedonica.* A deep maroon daylily would add interest, and certainly some early tulips, such as 'Queen of the Night', add even more colour. The bearded irises (available in many colours) would enhance the look, as would lilies. Chrysanthemums and sedums add pink and white, or violet foliage.

The beauty of a design like this is that it's difficult to make a mistake with such a carefully controlled palette. After making up the plant list, try moving the plants around (doing it on paper first should eliminate any potential problems) until you have a scheme based on the plants' eventual sizes. Don't line up all the plants of the same height on the same plane because that would be boring; pull a few forward and push others back.

It's also important to arrange the flowering times so that there are good combinations throughout the season. The easiest way to keep track of this is through tissue paper overlays showing what's in flower during each two-month period. Thus the tulips would flower in the spring overlay, the iris, salvias, heucheras and lilies in early summer, the daylilies and knautia in midsummer, and the chrysanthemums and sedums in the autumn overlay.

Also note that the smaller, alpine-derived heucheras are most suited to the rock garden, and that larger, taller varieties are best located in the border, as perennials. That shade-loving plants, including the tiarellas, prefer the woodland path or border. And that siting the plants correctly the first time saves you, and the plants, a lot of stress.

Alpines planted in a trough

Troughs require a special soil mix, very well drained and gritty. Set rocks as you would a miniature mountain, grouping them to good effect until the arrangement is pleasing. Plant the individual plants so that they do not touch other plants. They will gradually fill in.

1 *Heuchera* 'Petite Pearl Fairy'
2 *H. pulchella*
3 *H. elegans*
4 *H. hirsutissima*
5 *H. rubescens* 'Troy Boy'

6 *Dianthus* 'Tiny Rubies'
7 *Veronica* 'Waterperry'
8 *Thymus serpyllum* 'Mini'
9 *Phlox subulata* var. *brittonii*
10 *Antennaria dioica*

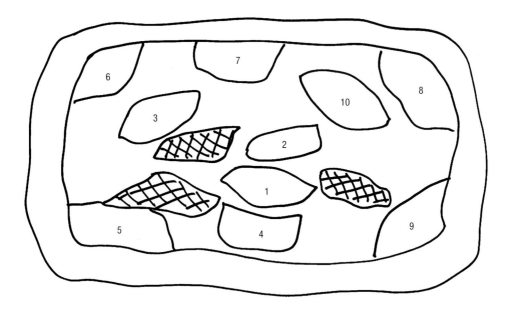

ROCK-GARDEN HEUCHERAS FOR SUNNY SITES

Heucheras in the 'Petite' Series, as well as the alpine types such as *H. hallii* and *H. pulchella*, all demand well-drained conditions and sun to thrive. The smaller Canyon hybrids and *H. elegans*, *H. hirsutissima* and *H. rubescens* 'Troy Boy' are also part of this group. They appreciate soil that's near neutral, which many rock gardens can supply. Adding coarse sand or gravel to the soil will greatly improve their survival rate, although they do appreciate some nourishment. They are best suited to troughs, containers and specially prepared raised beds (see Chapter 6). Rocks mean that the extensive root systems have to delve deep for the moisture and nutrients beneath,

keeping them warm in winter and cool in summer. Containers and beds can also be an attractive part of the design.

All these plants can be grown with small spring bulbs, *Phlox subulata brittonii*, tiny sedums, antennarias, small dianthus, veronicas, gentians or any of the delightful, tiny rock garden plants. For more information contact the North American Rock Garden Society (www.NARGS.org) or, in the UK, the Alpine Garden Society (www.alpinegarden society.org).

Other species and cultivars of heucheras, such as the larger Canyon hybrids and *H. pubescens* and *H. alba*, may be planted in the open garden, with the caveat that they require the good drainage and sunny conditions specified above. They can be combined with

Heuchera, Athyrium, Hosta

A sunny rock garden

Some gardeners devote a lifetime to the pursuit of perfection in the rock garden, trying to grow jewel-like alpines which demand perfect drainage, good air circulation and strong sun. The plants in this design are easier to grow and require less heartbreak. They are also visible to the naked eye from some distance away.

The rock arrangement pictured won't be duplicated in your setting; just arrange the rocks as they would be found in nature, buried partway in the ground with the most attractive side facing out (or up). Remember that rocks tend to line up in strata, and should be arranged this way.

Each rock becomes a shelter for its nearby plant, keeping the roots cool and moist and warming the soil in the spring. They also hold the heat in the cool days of autumn.

1 *Heuchera* 'Canyon Delight'	6 *Sedum sieboldii*
2 *H.* 'Canyon Pink'	7 *Cheilanthes lanosa*
3 *H.* 'Canyon Duet'	8 *Coreopsis* 'Moonbeam'
4 *H.* 'Petite Marbled Burgundy'	9 *Antennaria neglecta*
5 *H.* 'Chiqui'	10 *Dianthus allwoodii*

Heuchera 'Chiqui' in a rock garden in Newfoundland

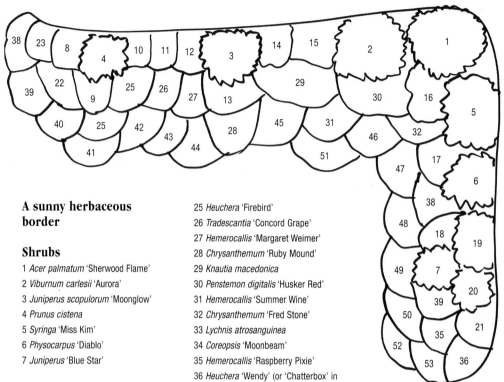

A sunny herbaceous border

Shrubs

1 *Acer palmatum* 'Sherwood Flame'
2 *Viburnum carlesii* 'Aurora'
3 *Juniperus scopulorum* 'Moonglow'
4 *Prunus cistena*
5 *Syringa* 'Miss Kim'
6 *Physocarpus* 'Diablo'
7 *Juniperus* 'Blue Star'

Tall perennials for the background

8 *Helenium autumnale*
9 *Lilium* 'Black Beauty'
10 *Chrysanthemum* x *superbum* 'Becky'
11 *Hibiscus* 'Sweet Caroline'
12 *Boltonia* 'Snowbank'
13 *Anemone robustissima*
14 *Phlox* 'Eva Cullum'
15 *Hibiscus* 'Luna Red'
16 *Phlox* 'David'
17 *Echinacea* 'Magnus'
18 *Aster* 'Bluebird'
19 *Buddleia* 'Nanho Blue' (cut to
  ground annually)
20 *Heliopsis* 'Lemon Queen'
21 *Nepeta* 'Six Hills Giant'

Medium height perennials for the middle

22 *Baptisia australis*
23 *Sedum* 'Autumn Joy'
24 *Gaura* 'Siskiyou Pink'

25 *Heuchera* 'Firebird'
26 *Tradescantia* 'Concord Grape'
27 *Hemerocallis* 'Margaret Weimer'
28 *Chrysanthemum* 'Ruby Mound'
29 *Knautia macedonica*
30 *Penstemon digitalis* 'Husker Red'
31 *Hemerocallis* 'Summer Wine'
32 *Chrysanthemum* 'Fred Stone'
33 *Lychnis atrosanguinea*
34 *Coreopsis* 'Moonbeam'
35 *Hemerocallis* 'Raspberry Pixie'
36 *Heuchera* 'Wendy' (or 'Chatterbox' in
  cold climate)
37 *Sedum* 'Neon'

Short perennials for the front

38 *Aster* 'Purple Dome'
39 *Heuchera* 'Quilters' Joy'
40 *Heuchera* 'Santa Ana Cardinal' (or
  hardier red cultivar in cold climate)
41 *Sedum* 'Vera Jamison'
42 *Aster frikartii* 'Wonder of Staffa'
43 *Salvia* 'East Frieslands'
44 *Heuchera* White Cloud
45 *Festuca* 'Elijah Blue'
46 *Heuchera* 'Coral Bouquet'
47 *Aster* 'Professor Kippenberg'
48 *Salvia officinalis* f. *purpurea*
49 *Heuchera* 'Rosemary Bloom'
50 *Nepeta* 'Walker's Low'
51 *Geranium sanguineum* var. *striatum*
52 *Dianthus* 'First Love'
53 *Thymus* 'Bressingham Pink'

Heuchera Brizoides in perennial border at Royal Botanic Garden, Edinburgh

the likes of opuntias, large *Phlox subulata,* campanulas such as *C. rotundifolia* and *C. poscharskyana, Coreopsis verticillata,* alliums, larger spring and summer bulbs, sempervivums, *Callirhoe involucrata,* small irises, larger dianthus, and thymes, etc. Like the smaller forms, they are mostly planted singly rather than in drifts, and they appear to do best when there is space around them and other plants aren't hovering over them or pushing them aside.

HEUCHERAS FOR SUNNY HERBACEOUS BORDERS

If the soil in the herbaceous border is well drained and neutral in pH, many of the larger cultivars may be used in a cottage garden scheme. *H.* 'Coral Bouquet' and all of the Brizoides types are used in this way by many gardeners. The Rancho Santa Ana hybrids can be especially lovely for massing, creating a mist of pink when seen from a distance, and the larger-flowered types may also be massed in groups. Use these plants to face down peonies or anchusas, tall campanulas or early bearded irises.

The effect created when tulips rise out of a sea of forget-me-nots can be echoed using a pink swarm of heucheras and adding pale yellow *Alchemilla mollis,* blue delphiniums or white Shasta daisies. They also marry well with tall veronicas or salvias, and may be used with other pink flowers to establish extra colour nuances. Try using dianthus, single late tulips, lilacs, armerias, aquilegias, lamium, lupins or early phlox, such as *P. divaricata* or *P. pilosa.* The good foliage is a plus in front of Oriental poppies and other plants with stems and leaves which deteriorate after flowering.

White-flowering forms, of which there are fewer, may be used the same way, to bring a lightness and airiness to the border. Gertrude Jekyll used white as a contrast and as part of a gradual intermingling of pastels in her borders, so you could use them with creamy thalictrums, bulb lilies or daisies, or pair them with bright pink and yellow as above.

Red-flowering forms also make wonderful additions to a sunny border. Few have delicate textures, but the same effect could be gained by using them with large red flowers such as achilleas or early bearded irises. There are fewer early summer-flowering reds than pinks.

HEUCHERAS FOR NATURALIZING IN SHADE

Heucheras that occur wild in shade (in deep woods or rocky crevices) are very adaptable to being used in sweeps or drifts as they sometimes occur in nature. (They also occur singly where conditions are especially challenging.) *H. americana* and *H. villosa* and the hybrids derived from them, with both purple and green leaves, may be planted informally and lavishly along woodland paths or in groups beside large rocks. They create summer interest, even when not in flower, adding foliage textures and colours.

Ferns are ideal companions because they are finer in texture, the very opposite of hostas. Hellebores of all kinds can be worked into the scheme, ephemeral native spring flora is always suitable, and tiarellas also make good companions. A design with such plants would be the easiest of all gardens to care for, and would be enduring. In a deciduous woodland, the primary maintenance would be removing the unwanted tree seedlings which would take just a few hours each year.

Ferns in the proper proportions to these heucheras tend to be the mid-sized ones: the wood fern (*Dryopteris carthusiana*), male fern (*Dryopteris felix-mas*) and Christmas fern

Heucheras naturalized with hostas

(*Polystichum acrostichoides*), etc. They are also the ones which can cope with dry shade under trees and among rocks when summer nutrients and moisture are at a premium. Hostas are also suitable for this site but, again, go for the mid-sized ones such as *H.* 'Halcyon', an old-fashioned type that's still one of the best, and the sweetly scented *H. plantaginea* 'Grandiflora', but avoid the huge *H. sieboldiana* 'Elegans'.

HEUCHERAS IN THE SHADY PERENNIAL BED

A more formal planting than naturalizing means that these plants really shine and show off what they can do. As suggested, both the green and the purple-leafed forms lend themselves to being massed in a bedding scheme. This arrangement is relatively easy to plan and very effective.

First, establish the size and shape of the bed, associating it with a major tree or shrub border if possible. Decide where the front and back are, which will influence your choices based on height. Put the tall plants in the background and the short ones to the front (the primary rule of traditional garden design). Then put in the garden paths, and if they can curve, enticing walkers on with hidden views, all the better.

But how many plants should you put in each group? A large garden might need a dozen plants, a smaller one only seven. Of course there can be 'drifts' of just one plant, as plantsman Tony Avent advocates, but you may end up with a plant collection rather than a garden.

The plant associations are so easy that one could almost call them foolproof. My first choices for shady companions are *Athyrium niponicum* f. *pictum* (the Japanese painted fern), and its associated forms such as 'Ursula's Red', lady ferns such as *Athyrium felix-femina* 'Lady in Red' and their mutual hybrids, 'Branford Beauty', 'Branford Rambler' and 'Ghost'. All are spectacular companions with the purple-leafed heucheras.

A naturalized shady woodland path

This is an easy garden to design, because it is based on a meandering path through the woods. Allow room for plenty of twists and turns in the path, leading the walker on. Use large groups of perennials, as many as you can get, and leave space between them; they will expand.

Shrubs suited to your site may be added, rhododendrons and azaleas if the soil is acid, viburnums and hydrangeas if it is alkaline or neutral. Small trees contribute to understory interest.

Ferns and hostas are most suited to this site because they are easy to care for, practically no maintenance, and they offer fine and coarse foliage to contrast with the heucheras and tiarellas. The right ones for the site (dry or moist) can be selected.

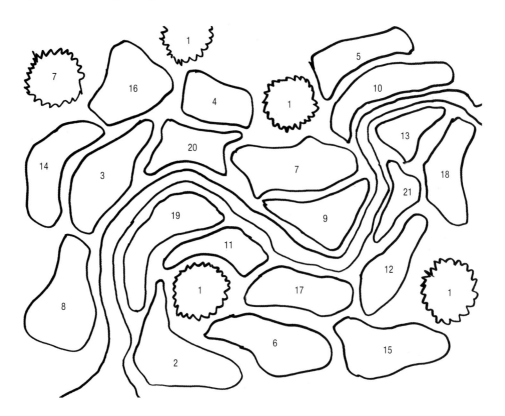

1 shrubs	8 *Tiarella* 'Martha Oliver'	15 *D. felix-mas*
2 *Heuchera americana* 'Green Spice'	9 *T. cordifolia* var. *cordifolia* wild type	16 *Hosta plantaginea* 'Grandiflora'
3 *H. a.* 'Eco-magnififolia'	10 *T.* 'Running Tiger'	17 *H.* 'Snowflake'
4 *H. a.* Dale's Strain	11 *T.* 'Running Tapestry'	18 *H. sieboldiana* 'Elegans'
5 *H. a.* 'Garnet'	12 *T.* 'Green Sword'	19 *Phlox stolonifera*
6 *H. villosa* 'Bronze Wave'	13 *Heucherella* 'Burnished Bronze'	20 *Mitella diphylla*
7 *H. v.* 'Molly Bush'	14 *Dryopteris carthusiana*	21 *M. stylosa*

A shady garden

Plants that enjoy dry shade, with well-drained soil or competition from tree roots, are both rare and sought-after. But under a beech or silver maple (or even the dreaded Norway maple) it is possible to grow a limited palette of plants which will survive these conditions. Be sure to do some soil improvement in the form of leaf mould or compost. If you do add a lot of humus, add some sand, too, the sharp, coarse kind, to prevent compacting and loss of air in the soil. Rocks are optional.

1 *Heuchera* Montrose Ruby
2 *H. villosa* 'Bronze Wave'
3 *H.* 'Regina'
4 *Epimedium* 'Frohnleiten'
5 *E. youngianum* 'Niveum'
6 *Dryopteris felix-mas*
7 *D. carthusiana*

8 *Tiarella cordifolia* var. *collina*
9 *T.* 'Pink Brushes'
10 *Sedum ternatum*
11 *Hosta* 'Halcyon'
12 *H.* 'Blue Cadet'
13 *H.* 'Blue Angel'
14 *Asarum splendens*

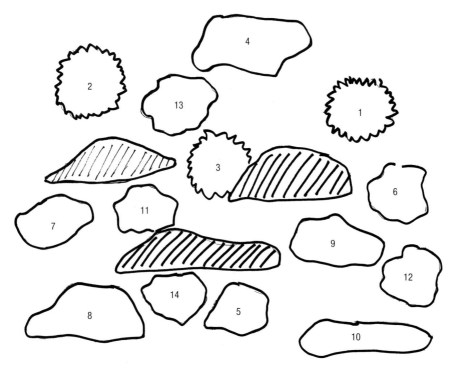

Keeping the same tones would call for a silver or blue hosta, such as 'Blue Cadet', 'June', or *H. sieboldiana*. Pulmonarias in the silver tones add a pleasing contrast. A similar colouring is found in the Asian ginger *Asarum splendens*. A contrast in leaf texture in green/silver could be added with the variegated sedge *Carex* 'Silver Scepter'. Make sure that the clumps are roughly equal in size, or in numbers of individual plants, and remember that uneven numbers are easier to place. Gertrude Jekyll advocated a group of plants making a shape with a point at each end, and a bulge in the middle, called an 'oblate spheroid'. After a few years the plants will have obliterated the carefully planned shapes, but will have come up with something very attractive on their own.

The well-drained, neutral soil will also support primroses, such as the Julian hybrids, in the bright maroon and fuchsia colours which resonate with heuchera leaves, especially as the new ones emerge in early spring. *Geranium phaeum* 'Samobor' reflects the purple leaves, and some of the dark-leafed sedums could be included.

www.plantagogo.com Order Form

Before placing your order, please read our terms and conditions at the front of our catalogue.
Thank You.

	QUANTITY	PLANT NAME	PRICE	TOTAL
1				
2				
3				
4				
5				
6				
7				
8				
9				
10				
11				
12				
13				
14				
15				
16				
17				
18				
19				
20				
21				
22				
23				
24				
25				
26				
27				
28				
29				
30				

Substitutes or State Alternatives		TOTAL	£
		POSTAGE	£7.95
Yes	No	TOTAL AMOUNT	£

D. R. & H.V. Fox, Jubilee Cottage Nursery
Snape Lane, Englesea Brook, Weston
Crewe, Cheshire, CW2 5QN
Tel/Fax: 01270 820335

www.plantagogo.com Order Form

Date of order: ⬜️⬜️⬜️⬜️   Name: ⬜️⬜️⬜️⬜️   (PLEASE USE BLOCK CAPITALS)

Address:

Post Code: Telephone:

E-mail:

⬜️ **I enclose cheque/postal order payable to D.R. & H.V. Fox**

⬜️ Please debit my Credit Card with the amount £ _____ details as follows:

⬜️ Visa   ⬜️ Mastercard/Access

⬜️ Switch

Issue Date: _____ / _____   Issue No.: _____   Security code on back of card: _____

Start Date: _____ / _____   Expiry Date: _____ / _____

Card Number: ⬜️⬜️⬜️⬜️ ⬜️⬜️⬜️⬜️ ⬜️⬜️⬜️⬜️ ⬜️⬜️⬜️⬜️

Signed by the Card Holder:

UK Mainland

One amount of **£7.95** for as many plants as you wish to order. So the more you order the better the deal becomes.

Any Other Destinations

Please contact us for a quote. Either by ringing **01270 820 335** or e-mailing us on **info@plantagogo.com**

When the plants arrive

All of our plants are ready for planting when dispatched unless otherwise stated.
Please unpack them carefully as soon as possible. If they are dry please water them.
Place them outside as soon as possible, unless otherwise stated.

All of our plants are supplied with colour labels where ever possible, and written labels when they are not available. This makes identification easy. Most of the labels will have growing and cultural notes on the reverse. However if you require more information please telephone or e-mail on above numbers.

PLEASE NOTE! Please make cheques etc. payable to D.R. & H.V. Fox.

A midwestern prairie planting

Prairies tend to be mixtures of plants, not arranged as to size at all, but as they grow naturally. *Heuchera richardsonii* is a typical prairie plant in this way, so arranging a planting of this sort is simple.

Plants which grow in association with *H. richardsonii* are the Midwestern native wildflowers and grasses. Although it is possible to start a prairie planting from seed, it is far more reliable to use plugs (small plants) which have been raised in a nursery bed.

Secure the site through ploughing or herbicides, and set out plants in the spring. Arrange the path structure and plant. It will be necessary to weed carefully the first several years, until the plants fill in the empty space and can be relied upon to smother weeds. After that an annual mowing or burning will keep out woody species.

Allium cernuum (nodding onion)	*Heuchera richardsonii* (Richardson's alum root)
Asclepias incarnata (pink milkweed)	*Liatris spicata* (blazing star)
Aster azureus (sky blue aster)	*Monarda fistulosa* (bergamot)
Aster laevis (smooth aster)	*Penstemon digitalis* (foxglove beard tongue)
Aster novae-angliae (New England aster)	*Ratabida pinnata* (yellow coneflower)
Baptisia australis (false indigo)	*Rudbeckia fulgida* (brown eyed susan)
Cassia hebecarpa (wild senna)	*Silphium laciniatum* (compass plant)
Coreopsis lanceolata (stiff coreopsis)	*Solidago ohioensis* (Ohio golden rod)
Echinacea purpurea (purple coneflower)	*Tradescantia ohioensis* (Ohio spiderwort)
Eupatorium fistulosum (Joe Pye weed)	*Vernonia noveboracensis* (ironweed)
Helianthus mollis (downy sunflower)	*Veronicastrum virginicum* (culver's root)
Helianthus helianthoides (false sunflower)	

COMPANION PLANTS FOR HEUCHERELLAS

The heucherellas prefer the cultural conditions of their tiarella rather than their heuchera parent; in other words, these plants prefer shade at least some of the time and moist, humus-rich soil. They combine well with moisture-loving ferns (ostrich, cinnamon and royal ferns) and hostas (hostas aren't choosy about moisture). All the native spring ephemerals may be planted with them. Use *Phlox stolonifera*, wild gingers, and of course tiarellas and *Mitella diphylla*.

Most will flower more reliably with extra nutrients, perhaps because they lack the storage capacity of their parents, but when well fed they are beautiful. Astilbes are good companions that appreciate the extra moisture and nutrients. Add some aruncus and cimicifugas for bottlebrush-type flowers. Clethra also enjoys these conditions, and produces a similar flower spike, as does *Pachysandra procumbens*. Add vancouveria as good ground cover.

Some suggested combinations and rough garden designs are on pages 52–62, and can be adapted to other sites quite easily. The formal border (which is square or rectangular), the island bed (which may or may not surround a tree or shrub), and the freeform drift are all pictured and delineated. Modify them as your needs dictate.

THE BEST CHOICES FOR THE GARDEN

The plants in this section have been chosen on the basis of being the most attractive, vigorous, and dependable examples of the various groupings by garden use that we discussed in Chapter 2. We have tried to consider usefulness in plant combinations and designs, as well as availability. Most plant source lists in gardening books are out of date before the books appear in print, but the *RHS Plant Finder* is a notable exception, and is an excellent source list in the UK. In North America the best source is the Internet. Most mail-order nurseries keep their lists up to date, and many garden centres post their spring inventories on the Web. We search for plants using Google, and avoid using business directories or search engines where companies need to pay to be included, which rules out most of the small specialist nurseries. Many botanic gardens and state agricultural agencies though, do put their source lists on the Web.

The following profiles include plants that have been awarded a Royal Horticultural Society Award of Garden Merit, indicated by (AGM). It is awarded after garden trials at the RHS headquarters at Wisley in Surrey. Any given plant genus is judged at intervals of some years, and heucheras were last judged in 2001. The lack of many awards in the group may mean simply that a given cultivar was not on the market when the trials started, or was not submitted for the trials.

Plants vary in how well they adapt to growth in full sun. We have noted varieties that seem to be especially sun-resistant in our gardens, but this will be different in other climates (see Chapter 6). Most of the alpine heucheras and the larger rock garden types should cope with full sun in cooler climates and with adequate moisture, although they will probably be happier with light shade in the afternoon. The other types probably need some sun protection except as noted.

Heuchera pulchella

Heuchera – for rock gardens, containers, troughs and special beds

H. pulchella

Description: This wild species is found on limestone cliffs in the mountains of central New Mexico at 2450–3260m (8050–10,700ft). It makes a widening clump of smooth, rounded and scalloped evenly green leaves, 3cm (1¼in) wide, that becomes 10cm (4in) high and 25cm (10in) wide after two years. The tufty growth habit is quite different from that of the mat-forming species like *H. rubescens* and the southern California species (see below). Upright 20–25cm (8–10in) inflorescences appear in mid-spring. The flowers are about 5mm (0.19in) long, resembling a baggy tube narrowed at the end. The stamens project from the mouth of the calyx, giving a frilly appearance. Flower colour varies from dingy pinkish-white to very attractive pinks and, since no selections seem to have been made in the species, it is worthwhile growing a group of plants from seed to choose the best flower colours.

Special qualities: *H. pulchella* is an easy and adaptable species that flowers abundantly under lowland rock garden conditions. It is the showiest of the Rocky Mountain wild species. An especially good plant of this species was given to us in the early 1990s by Panayoti Kelaidis, Curator of the Denver Botanic Garden Rock Garden. This individual was one of the grandparents of the Petite Series of heucheras.

Availability: Plants of *H. pulchella* can be obtained from many specialist nurseries. Seed is often available from society exchanges and alpine seed dealers.

'Petite Pearl Fairy'

Description: This little cultivar has rounded, scalloped leaves about 3.5cm (1½in) across, and makes a mound of foliage about 10cm (4in) tall and 20cm (8in) across in two years. Plants quickly become multicrowned, but remain in a single dense clump, like *H. pulchella*. The leaves are bronze patterned with silver, becoming bronze-green in summer. In mid-spring there are upright stems of 5mm (0.19in) long flowers to 30cm (12in) high. The flowers have light pink calyces and projecting, recurved white petals. It was a 1997 introduction from The Primrose Path.

Special qualities: 'Petite Pearl Fairy' is the only one of the new bronze and silver foliage hybrids that is as small as the diminutive alpine species, and suitable for trough use. The RHS Wisley Trials noted that this had the best foliage of any of the rock garden heucheras.

Availability: 'Petite Pearl Fairy' is probably the most widely available of the small heucheras, and can be obtained from many nurseries in North America and Europe.

'Petite Marbled Burgundy'

Description: Grown under lean rock gardens conditions, 'Petite Marbled Burgundy' forms a mound of foliage about 12cm (4½in) high and 20cm (8in) across in two years. The leaves are 3.5–4cm (1½–1¾in) across, and bronze-purple patterned with silver. In spring there are abundant, nearly spherical flowers about 5mm (0.19in) long that have pink calyces and white projecting petals, and are borne on upright, sturdy stems to about 35cm (14in) high. When well fed, plants are somewhat larger, with inflorescences to about 45cm (18in) and leaves up to 7cm (2¾in) across. The caudex of this cultivar is especially thick and the leaves are heavy-textured. As plants mature, relatively few, larger offsets are produced compared with 'Petite Pearl Fairy.' This was a 1997 introduction from The Primrose Path.

Special qualities: 'Petite Marbled Burgundy' is one of the showiest of the small heuchera cultivars. It is very adaptable, suitable for different garden uses, from containers or special raised beds to front of the border.

Availability: Generally available in North America and Europe.

H. elegans and H. hirsutissima

Description: These two wild species are very similar overall, the species differing botanically only in minor flower characteristics. Both grow as widening mats of foliage rosettes, a very different habit from that of *H. pulchella* and its grandchildren, the Petite hybrids. Our garden plants of *H. elegans* are smaller and tighter growing than those of *H. hirsutissima*, which are the selection 'Santa Rosa.' Our clump of *H. elegans* has become 4cm (1¾in) high by 12cm (4½in) wide over two years, while *H. hirsutissima* is 6cm (2½in) tall by 20cm (8in) wide. Both have leaves about 15mm (0.6in) across, but those of *H. elegans* are less hairy. Both flower in mid-spring and

have outfacing, flared tubular flowers 6–7mm (0.2–0.3in) long with pink calyces and white petals, in irregular, 25cm (10in) sprays. These two species, and others closely related, are native to the mountains of southern California. Since they grow at altitudes of 1385–3500m (4500–11,500ft) they are winter hardy to about USDA Zone 4. These species have been combined with *H. sanguinea* hybrids (i.e. Brizoides) to produce the Canyon hybrids (see below).

Left *Heuchera* 'Petite Pearl Fairy'
Below *Heuchera* 'Petite Marbled Burgundy'

Heuchera elegans in the San Gabriel Mountains, California
(Photo by Tom Chester)

Special qualities: These species grow so as to fill spaces between rocks with a solid expanse of low foliage. The flowers appear as a cloud of pale pink. The colour is less intense and the panicles are more open and irregular than in the selected Canyon hybrids, but these wild species are very beautiful plants. The selection *H. hirsutissima* 'Santa Rosa' has flowers that are sweet-scented and very vivid.

Availability: Plants can be found at a few specialist alpine nurseries in North America. Seed is usually available from society exchanges.

Small Canyon hybrids
Description: All form rosettes of slightly hairy, 2–3cm (¾–1¼in) wide leaves, and grow as slowly expanding mats usually 6–8cm (2½–3½in) high. 'Blushing Bells' (*H. merriamii* x Brizoides) has pale pink flowers on 20–30cm (8–12in) long stems. 'Canyon Chimes' (a back-cross of *H. elegans* x Brizoides to *H. elegans*) has dark pink flowers on taller stems.

'Dainty Bells' (*H. hirsutissima* x Brizoides) has rose-pink flowers stems to about 30cm (12in) long. 'Pink Wave' (an F2 hybrid of *H. elegans* and Brizoides) has rose-pink flowers to about 30cm (12in) from a mat only 3–5cm (¾–2in) high. The flowers of these hybrids are of solid colours, rather than the bicolours of the California wild parents, and lack the flared tube shape. The flower panicles tend to be more regular in shape. They were introduced by the Santa Barbara Botanic Garden in the late 1990s.

Special qualities: These are the smallest hybrid garden heucheras, and they bring a greater range of flower form and colour to the heucheras grown in containers. At the Santa Barbara Botanic Garden many of the smaller Canyon hybrids are grown in open beds in the shade of large trees, and we noted that the plants in containers were flowering much more heavily than those in open ground.

Availability: They can be obtained mainly from specialized nurseries dealing in alpines or California native plants.

H. rubescens 'Troy Boy'
Description: The species has a wide geographic range in western North America,

Heuchera rubescens 'Troy Boy'

Heuchera 'Pink Wave' at the Santa Barbara Botanic Garden, California

and varies greatly in size and growth habit. The larger forms are less attractive as garden plants than the other alpine types we have included because of their smaller, less showy flowers. 'Troy Boy' is worth growing for its foliage alone, and makes a low, even mat of smooth, dark green 1.5cm (0.6in) wide leaves. Our three-year-old plant is 4cm (1¾in) tall and 20cm (8in) across. It flowers in mid-spring with 5mm (0.19in) long, greenish-white flowers that turn pinkish with age and are borne on sparsely produced 12cm (4½in) long stems. This selection was made from Troy Peak in the Charleston Mountains of Nevada by the late Roy Davidson, and is probably the smallest heuchera grown in gardens. There are other very small forms with better flowers:

a plant we saw labelled as *Heuchera rubescens* in a trough at the Edinburgh Botanical Garden in Scotland had abundant intensely pink flowers on stems about 10cm (4in) tall.

Special qualities: 'Troy Boy' has proved to be exceptionally resistant to summer heat and humidity in western Pennsylvania. The foliage has not been subject to die-back from fungus attacks, and shows no evidence of slug damage even though heucheras near it have been chewed.

Availability: 'Troy Boy' is available at some specialist nurseries in North America. Seed of *H. rubescens* is available from society exchanges. Alpine nurseries in the UK may have good forms of *H. rubescens* other than 'Troy Boy'.

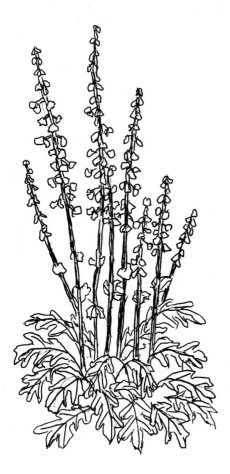

Special qualities: The larger Canyon hybrids are similar in overall size to the Petite hybrids but have a rather different form. The foliage is more compact, and the flower stems appear longer. The flower sprays are more diffuse and airy, and the individual flowers smaller.

Availability: They can be found in the lists of many mail order nurseries in North America and a few in the UK.

H. 'Coral Bouquet' and H. 'Chiqui'

Description: These two cultivars resemble each other since each has large, shrimp-pink flowers and a tuft of green foliage. 'Coral Bouquet' has smoother green leaves patterned with silver, being about 5cm (2in) across, and relatively dense, 15cm (6in) long panicles of 9mm (0.35in) long flowers on 45–55cm (18–22in) long stems. The leaves of 'Chiqui' are a little larger, about 6cm (2½in) across, lightly marked with silver, and hairier; its flowers are a little wider and shorter, appearing in looser, sparser panicles on 55cm (20in) long stems. 'Coral Bouquet' is our earliest flowering heuchera, often starting by late April. 'Chiqui' flowers a couple of weeks later. Both make a foliage clump about 12cm (4½in) high and 30cm (12in) across. 'Coral Bouquet' and 'Chiqui' are both selections from the hybrid cross *H. cylindrica* x Brizoides. 'Chiqui' was introduced by George Schenk in 1989, and 'Coral Bouquet' by The Primrose Path in 1997.

Special qualities: These cultivars have especially large and showy flowers, and 'Coral Bouquet' has a very long flowering period. The cultivars are also suitable for formal displays in well-drained soil. Both cultivars usually do well in full sun if it is not too hot.

Availability: Both are available from mail-order nurseries.

H. pubescens and H. alba

Description: *H. pubescens*, of the central Appalachians, is a medium-sized heuchera

Heuchera – rock garden: for the open garden

Larger Canyon hybrids

Description: These selections from the Santa Barbara Botanic Garden are very attractive when they are used in large containers, but also do well in open gardens. 'Canyon Pink', a back-cross of *H. elegans* x Brizoides to *H. elegans*, has leaves about 5cm (2in) wide and medium pink flowers on 30cm (12in) long stems. 'Canyon Delight', an F1 *H. elegans* x Brizoides hybrid, is one of the best known and has dark rose-red flowers on a plant of similar size. 'Canyon Duet' is a back-cross of 'Canyon Delight' to *H. elegans*, and has pink and white flowers on 30–45cm (12–18in) long stems. It resembles the wild *H. elegans* more than the other hybrids.

Campanula patula
var. dasyantha

Heuchera X
'Chiqui'

with angular leaves from 8–12cm (3½–4½in) across, in a mound about 25cm (10in) high by 40cm (16in) wide. In spite of the name, the foliage is almost smooth to the touch. In late spring it has panicles of bells about 6mm (0.2in) wide and 9–10mm (0.35–0.4in) long, being borne on erect stems to 60cm (24in). Good forms of *H. pubescens* have decorative silver patterning on the leaves, contrasting reddish leaf petioles and flower stems, and large flowers of luminous pale green with white or purple petals. *H. alba*, from the Appalachian mountain tops, is similar but more compact, with more flowers on shorter inflorescences and larger flowers to 1.3cm (0.5in) long. Good forms have flowers of creamy white and contrastingly reddish petioles and flower stems. Both species have

Heuchera 'Canyon Delight' at the Santa Barbara Botanic Garden, California

Heuchera pubescens at Greenland Gap, West Virginia

Heuchera alba at Spruce Knob, West Virginia

been heavily used in the heuchera breeding programme at The Primrose Path.

Special qualities: These species have the largest flowers in the genus *Heuchera*, are very hardy and easy to grow. They are unlike any of the other wild heucheras in appearance, and make an interesting addition to a rock garden. They should grow well in full sun if the summer is not very hot and dry.

Problems: Slug and snail damage may be extensive on the foliage. This commonly occurs in nature on *H. pubescens* but seems to do little harm. *H. alba* needs good air circulation and good drainage to prevent fungus damage during hot, humid periods in the summer.

Availability: These plants are most commonly available as seed distributed by rock garden societies. It is best to grow from seed, anyway, so that the most garden-worthy plants can be selected from a group of seedlings. *H. alba* has a very small geographic range, and should not be collected as seed or plants. It is on global and North American state and federal endangered lists. Seed is distributed by some botanic gardens.

Heuchera – for naturalizing

H. americana

Description: *H. americana* (alum root), has slightly hairy leaves that are more rounded in outline than those of *H. pubescens*, being about 8–10cm (3½–4in) across. The foliage forms a loose mound about 25cm (10in) high and 30–40cm (12–16in) across. Tiny green flowers are borne in late spring at the top of upright stems 50–90cm (20–36in) tall. Selections of *H. americana* are similar to the wild species in overall size, habit and inflorescence.

Special qualities: *H. americana* can be used in natural settings in light shade, or in more formal beds where the flower stems are best removed. Since *H. americana* is tolerant of a wide range of soil pH, it can be used in colourful herbaceous plantings among acid-loving shrubs. The colour intensity and hue of the foliage of the best selected forms is probably unique in the wild temperate flora. 'Garnet' is a selection whose leaf is almost entirely maroon in the spring, fading to green

over summer. It was introduced by the Mount Cuba Center for the Study of Piedmont Flora near Wilmington, Delaware, and is used in native plantings there.

Dale's Strain is a seed strain derived from plants with extensive silvering on the leaves which were found in the southern Appalachians by Dale Hendricks of North Creek Nurseries. The oddly named 'Eco-magnififolia' from Eco Gardens in Georgia (new Latinized cultivar names were banned many years ago and, in any case, the name would mean that the plant had large rather than 'magnificent' leaves) is a very good form that combines extensive silvering with bluish tones and maroon veining. It is planted in the Rhododendron Collection at the Holden Arboretum near Cleveland, Ohio. 'Green Spice', introduced by Terra Nova as 'Eco Improved', but not surprisingly renamed, is quite similar. *H. americana* grows well in full sun for us.

Availability: *H. americana* cultivars are very generally available at garden centres and from mail-order nurseries.

H. villosa

Description: This is the largest of the heucheras in general garden use. Plants are variable in size, depending on genetics and growing conditions. The leaves are large, acutely lobed, and up to 20cm (8in) wide. Plants grown under good conditions will form a foliage mound 40cm (16in) high by 60–70cm (24–27in) wide. There are decorative, airy sprays of small, 3–4mm (0.1–0.15in) long whitish flowers on arching 70cm (27in) long stems in mid- to late summer. The leaf petioles and flower stems are covered with a whitish fuzz.

Special qualities: We have found *H. villosa* to be very hardy and tolerant of dry shade and tree roots, and adaptable to a wide range of soil types. It can be used in large plantings in light shade, where the bold foliage makes a refreshing alternative or complement to hostas. There are massed plantings of the wild-type form at Longwood Gardens in eastern Pennsylvania, and at the University of North Carolina Botanic Garden in Chapel Hill. 'Bronze Wave' is an especially large plant with thick stems and colour-retentive bronze-purple foliage with a slightly undulating leaf surface. It's a selection made at The Primrose Path from seed produced by plants of the type referred to as 'var. *macrorhiza*' from Tennessee, though the name is considered invalid by some

Heuchera americana Dale's Strain

authors. 'Molly Bush' is an especially good colour-retentive dark bronze selection from seed of Palace Purple. It was made by Allan Bush at Holbrook Nursery, and named after his daughter. This, like Palace Purple, is about two-thirds the size of 'Bronze Wave'.

Problems: *H. villosa* will survive in full sun in northern North America, but the foliage will be scorched.

Availability: These two selections have not yet become widely available. North Creek Nursery is one source. If Palace Purple must be used, it is worth buying seed of a selected strain and choosing the best individuals for propagation.

H. richardsonii

Description: This prairie species has rounded, hairy leaves about 10cm (4in) wide in a clump up to 50cm (20in) wide and 30cm (12in) tall. Like other species heucheras, the size depends greatly on the growing conditions. It flowers in early summer when small green flowers are borne on upright stems to 1m (3½ft) tall. The flowers are more interesting than decorative;

Left *Heuchera americana* 'Eco-magnififolia' at the Holden Arboretum, Ohio
Below *Heuchera villosa* 'Molly Bush'

Above *Heuchera villosa* 'Bronze Wave'
Right *Heuchera richardsonii* used in a formal bed in Pittsburgh, Pennsylvania

the stems can be trimmed off when the flowers begin to fade.

Special qualities: *H. richardsonii* is a very tough, hardy plant. It has been used as a basic part of the heuchera breeding programme at the Morden Research Station in Manitoba, whose goal was Brizoides-type heuchera hybrids hardy enough for general garden use in Canada. Well-grown plants of *H. richardsonii* are statuesque and handsome even without the dramatic foliage colouring of the other species and hybrids. It grows well for us in full sun.

Availability: Plants can be found at a few specialist nurseries. Seed is often available through exchanges.

Heuchera – for use in formal beds

Brizoides ('Firebird', 'Rosemary Bloom', White Cloud)

Description: These three selections are our favourites from this group. 'Firebird' (introduced by Blooms in the 1950s) has even, glossy green leaves about 6cm (2⅖in) across, forming a foliage mound about 20cm (8in) tall and 30cm (12in) across. The bright red flowers reach about 50cm (20in) high. 'Rosemary Bloom' has silver-patterned foliage of the same proportions and inflorescences to 60cm (24in) high. The clear pink flowers are large, being about 9mm (0.35in) long. This is a recent Blooms introduction, and named after the wife of Adrian Bloom. White Cloud has been marketed as a seed strain, and has large white flowers on 70cm (27in) stems, and silver-patterned leaves about 7cm (2¾in) across in a mound about the same size as the others.

Special qualities: These three have especially showy flowers, attractive foliage, and excellent vigour. They will grow in full sun, except in areas with very hot summers.

Availability: These, or very similar Brizoides cultivars, are readily obtained from garden centres or mail-order nurseries.

'Frosted Violet'

Description: 'Frosted Violet' forms a loose foliage mound about 25cm (10in) high and 40cm (16in) across. The sharp-lobed leaves resemble those of *H. villosa* f. *purpurea* cultivars, except that they are 8cm (3½in) wide as opposed to 10cm (4in). The foliage has a very unusual and striking colour, being purple-bronze marked with silvery pink-violet. This fades to purple and silver in the summer, and becomes dark bluish-purple and silver in the winter. Plants flower all summer with airy wands of small, 4mm (0.15in) long pink flowers on arching stems 60–70cm (14–27in) long. The young flower stems are covered with a decorative dense purple fuzz, and resemble pipe cleaners. This is a cross between *H. villosa* 'Bronze Wave' and *H.* 'Silver Lode' made at The Primrose Path in 1998.

Heuchera 'Firebird' at the Royal Botanic Garden, Edinburgh

Above *Heuchera* 'Rosemary Bloom'
Right *Heuchera* 'Wendy' at the Rancho Santa Ana Botanic Garden, California

Special qualities – 'Frosted Violet' has a late and long flowering period, flowering after most other garden cultivars have finished, and its colour is unique. Although Montrose Ruby, the original hybrid that combined bronze and silver foliage colour, involved *H. villosa*, this species has not been used as a parent in the newer hybrids except for 'Frosted Violet'.

Problems: 'Frosted Violet' should be grown in a site where there is some protection from sun in the hottest part of the day. Unless there is a dependable source of moisture, the foliage may develop brown scorch marks.

Availability: 'Frosted Violet' is becoming one of the best-selling heucheras in North America. It should soon be readily available in European outlets.

Heuchera 'Frosted Violet'

Rancho Santa Ana hybrids ('Wendy', 'Santa Ana Cardinal')

Description: We think that these two cultivars – 'Wendy' is pink and 'Santa Ana Cardinal' red – are probably the best of the *H. maxima* x *H. sanguinea* hybrids that have been developed at the Rancho Santa Ana Botanic Garden, California. These have rounded, somewhat hairy leaves slightly mottled with lighter colouration and are about 7–8cm (2¾–3⅛in) across in a mound about 25cm (10in) high and 35cm (14in) across. The flowers are straight-sided bells about 6mm (0.2in) long in large panicles to about 60cm (24in) high. Compared to the larger Brizoides cultivars, the Santa Ana hybrids have a more open, diffuse flower quality. At the Rancho Santa Ana Botanic Garden, and in other places in California, they are used to great effect as massed plantings of single cultivars, but we have not seen them used in formal schemes that depend on colours and textures.

Special qualities: The Rancho Santa Ana selections, like *H. maxima*, are drought-resistant and can be grown in dry summer spells without regular watering. Their flowers should make them useful in different ways to the other heucheras of similar size in this section.

Problems: The plants are winter-hardy only to about -10°C (14°F) and so are most suitable for garden use in mild climates. In cold climates they could be used in large container plantings protected from winter conditions. These appeared to us to grow better in light shade than sun in southern California.

Availability: They are available from many Pacific Coast nurseries in California and the Pacific Northwest, but we have not seen them for sale in Europe.

Montrose Ruby

Description: Our clone of this seed strain has angular leaves 15–17cm (6–6½in) wide, in an open mound about 25cm (10in) high and 45cm (18in) wide. There are thin panicles of tiny whitish flowers about 3mm (0.1in) long on arching stems to 70cm (27in) in midsummer. The spring foliage is a rich red-purple colour, heavily patterned with grey-silver. It was introduced in the mid-1980s by Montrose Nursery in North Carolina.

Special qualities: Montrose Ruby has an especially good red hue to the foliage that is not often seen in the later hybrids that have been bred from it. It's the first of the hybrids combining the bronze of *H. villosa* and the silver of *H. americana*, and it has a degree of vigour and endurance that has been lost in many of the newer hybrids. Some of our plants are naturalized in open woods, and they continue to thrive year after year with almost no care.

Availability: It can be found at many mail-order nurseries in North America and at a few in the UK.

Heuchera 'Santa Ana Cardinal' at the Rancho Santa Ana Botanic Garden, California

'Moonlight'

Description: This new hybrid has contrastingly chequered purple and silver leaves about 8cm (3½in) across, and a foliage mound about 20cm (8in) high and 30cm (12in) across. The flowers are wide, luminous, pale green bells about 9mm (0.35in) long on erect stems 40–50cm (16–20in) tall. The contrasting flower stems and their branches are very dark maroon. 'Moonlight' is from a cross made in 1999 at The Primrose Path between 'Silver Maps' (a sibling of 'Silver Scrolls' and 'Raspberry Ice') and a selected individual of *H. alba*.

Special qualities: 'Moonlight' is the first of the new hybrids that combines very large,

Above *Heuchera* 'Moonlight'
Left *Heuchera* Montrose Ruby

showy flowers with purple and silver foliage. The colour gives it a mysterious quality not seen before in a heuchera.

Availability: It should be available soon from mail-order nurseries.

'Obsidian'

Description: This new hybrid has smooth, glossy, evenly coloured foliage that is dark plum purple early in the season and turns dark green over summer. The leaves are rounded and about 10cm (4in) across in a clump 25cm (10in) high and 40cm (16in) wide. The flowers are tiny and cream-coloured in 50–60cm (20–24in) sprays in early summer.

Special qualities: 'Obsidian' is probably Terra Nova's best heuchera. It has a rich dark colour not seen in any other heuchera, and maintains

that even under hot, humid conditions. It has been very vigorous for us. The flowers are not showy, and are on relatively short, erect stems that do not detract from the foliage clump.

Availability: This is generally available from well-stocked garden centres and mail-order nurseries.

'Plum Pudding'

Description: The foliage is glossy beet-purple with indistinct silvery patterning. The leaves are deeply lobed and about 8cm (3½in) wide, and form an open mound 25cm high (10in) and 35cm (14in) wide. Insignificant flowers are borne in late spring on lanky 65cm (25in) stems, which it is best to remove. 'Plum Pudding' was introduced by Terra Nova in 1996.

Special qualities: The foliage of 'Plum Pudding' has an unusual 'shimmery' quality because of the way that its indistinct silvering and glossiness combine. It has become one of the standard heucheras.

Availability: It is generally available from garden centres and mail-order nurseries.

'Purple Petticoats' AGM

Description: 'Purple Petticoats' has evenly bronze-purple, highly ruffled leaves about 8cm (3½in) across in a clump 25cm (10in) high and 40cm (16in) across. There are tiny cream-coloured flowers on 60cm (24in) long stems in late spring. 'Purple Petticoats' was introduced by Terra Nova in 1997.

Special qualities: This has been the best of the ruffled heucheras that we have grown. It is

Left *Heuchera* 'Obsidian'
Below *Heuchera* 'Plum Pudding'

very winter-hardy and retains its colour well in summer heat.

Availability: At many garden centres and mail-order nurseries.

'Quilters' Joy' AGM

Description: 'Quilters' Joy' has deeply lobed leaves about 8cm (3½in) across which are crisply patterned in dark bronze and silver, giving a patchwork effect. It forms a foliage clump 20cm (8in) high and 35cm (14in) wide. In late spring there are 5mm (0.19in) long white flowers on erect 60cm (24in) high stems.

Special qualities: This early Primrose Path hybrid was a cross between 'White Marble' and Montrose Ruby, and it shows the vigour and endurance of the wild-type plants that were its grandparents. It has been especially adaptable for full sun in Pennsylvania.

Availability: 'Quilters' Joy' is available from many mail-order nurseries.

'Raspberry Ice'

Description: A sister of 'Silver Scrolls', 'Raspberry Ice' has more acutely lobed leaves about 8cm (3½in) across with a crisp pattern of metallic silver on purple-bronze. Well-fed plants will reach a size of about 25cm (10in) high and 50cm (20in) across. There are good pink flowers of substantial size, about 6mm

Below *Heuchera* 'Purple Petticoats' at the Center for Conservation Education, Westmoreland County, Pennsylvania

Right *Heuchera* 'Raspberry Ice' (Photo by Jane Grushow, used courtesy of Blooms of Bressingham)
Below *Heuchera* 'Quilters' Joy'

Heuchera 'Regina'

(0.2in) long, on erect 40cm (16in) long stems in late spring. It was introduced by The Primrose Path in 2002.

Special qualities: 'Raspberry Ice' combines highly silvered purple-bronze foliage with good pink flowers. It has an especially long flowering period, and was given a Classic City Award in 2004 by Allan Armitage for its excellent performance (16 weeks in flower) at the University of Georgia perennial trials.

'Regina' AGM

Description: 'Regina' has round-lobed, angular leaves about 10cm (4in) across with a red-purple background overlain with silvery patterning, and an all-over metallic sheen. The foliage reaches about 25cm (10in) high by 40cm (16in) wide. In late spring there are small, 5mm (0.19in) long, light pink, straight-sided bell flowers on 80cm (31in) long stems. The earliest of the silver and bronze hybrids with pink flowers, it was a 1997 introduction from The Primrose Path.

Special qualities: 'Regina' shows the endurance and vigour of the very early hybrids in this group. It has done well for us in full sun. This won a first prize at the Royal Society for Horticulture exposition in the Netherlands.

Availability: It is generally available from garden centres and mail-order nurseries.

'Silver Scrolls'

Description: The leaves of 'Silver Scrolls' are rounded and about 8cm (3½in) across. The upper leaf surface has an almost black-and-white effect: it's metallic silver with a highly contrasting scrollwork of crisp, dark bronze veins. The lower leaf surface is the even, dark red-purple of the other bronze foliage cultivars. In spring the new foliage is flushed with pink-purple. The foliage mound is about 15cm (6in) high and 35cm (14in) across. In late spring there are medium-sized white flowers from pink buds, to 65cm (25in) high in narrow panicles. Introduced by The Primrose Path in 1999.

Special qualities: The crisp metallic and dark leaf pattern of 'Silver Scrolls' is unique. It has done well in full sun in our area. 'Silver Scrolls' won a bronze medal at Plantarium 2000 in Holland.

Availability: This cultivar can be found at most good garden centres and mail-order nurseries.

Heuchera 'Silver Scrolls' at Shadowwood Nursery, Pennsylvania

Heucherella

The following four cultivars that we have chosen show the range of growth forms and foliage colours in these hybrids. They are plants that will do well in the garden over a long time if cared for properly, but they do require good soil fertility and reliable moisture to grow well.

'Burnished Bronze'

Description: It has glossy, brown-bronze, deeply lobed leaves about 10cm (4in) across in a tight mound about 20cm (8in) high and 35cm (14in) wide. In spring the leaves are a nearly even chocolate colour, but by summer the bronze fades enough to reveal a central medallion of darker maroon similar to that of many tiarellas. In late spring there are small light pink flowers in spikes (again, like a tiarella) borne on 45cm (18in) long stems. 'Burnished Bronze' was introduced by Terra Nova in 1999.
Special qualities: 'Burnished Bronze' makes an especially good dense foliage mound. The

bronze colour is retained well even in heat and dryness. 'Chocolate Lace' is a very similar newer cultivar, but it has not retained its colour as well for us during the summer.

'Heart of Darkness'

Description: The round-lobed leaves are about 8cm (3½in) across and have a patch of maroon in the centre, surrounded by silver, surrounded in turn by green. The dark coloration is seasonally variable, being most extensive in the spring foliage but fading in the summer. There are open, 50cm (20in) high branching sprays of medium-sized – 13mm (0.5in) wide by 6mm (0.2in) deep – white flowers in late spring, over 20cm (8in) high by 35cm (14in) wide clumps. It was introduced by The Primrose Path in 2002.
Special qualities: 'Heart of Darkness' has unusual green–silver–maroon coloration combined with abundant and showy flowers. When well-grown it is one of the largest of the heucherellas.
Availability: It can be obtained from many mail-order nurseries in North America, and will soon be available in Europe.

'Kimono' AGM

Description: This hybrid, between *H.* 'Green Spice' and a tiarella with deeply lobed foliage, has leaves 10–12cm (4–4¾in) across that are deeply and jaggedly lobed, with the central lobe extended in the manner of *T.* 'Green Sword'. The leaves have a silvery green ground colour, with a prominent central maroon blotch that extends out along the veins. The foliage colour fades to green over summer. The plants form a clump about 20cm (8in) high and 30cm (12in) wide. Small greenish-cream flowers are borne on lax, 40cm (16in) long stems in late spring, and do not add to the appearance of the plants. It was introduced by Terra Nova in 1999.
Special qualities: 'Kimono' has a unique combination of leaf colour and shape. It is the sort of plant that is most effective used singly or in a small group.
Availability: Available from many nurseries in North America and Europe.

Heucherella 'Heart of Darkness'

Top *Heucherella* 'Burnished Bronze'

Above *Heucherella* 'Kimono' (Photo by Dan Heims, Terra Nova Nurseries)

'Quicksilver'

Description: 'Quicksilver' has rounded, bronze leaves patterned with and overlain by metallic silver. The leaves are about 7cm (2¾in) across and form a clump 15cm (6in) high and 30cm (12in) wide. The medium-sized, pale pink, showy flowers reach about 40cm (16in) high, and age to white; opening from pink buds in inflorescences like those of a tiarella. The foliage colour changes from dark bronze in the spring to a silvery jade in the summer. 'Quicksilver' was introduced in 1997 by The Primrose Path.

Special qualities – This was the first of the 'new' heucherellas (i.e. with a heuchera parent of the purple-leafed hybrids descended from Montrose Ruby) to be bred, and it remains one of the most vigorous, reliable and attractive. The parental cross was done by us in 1993, and involved a heuchera that was a sibling of 'Quilters' Joy' and *Tiarella wherryi*.

Availability: Commonly available at nurseries.

Left *Heucherella* 'Quicksilver'
Below *Tiarella cordifolia* var. *cordifolia*

Tiarella

T. cordifolia var. cordifolia AGM and var. collina

Description: The wild forms of the running and non-running varieties of *T. cordifolia* are well worth growing in a natural setting. Var. cordifolia has heart-shaped leaves 6–8cm (2½–3½in) across, and makes an open mat 10–15cm (4–6in) wide with upright spikes of white or pale pink flowers. Even in wild populations there are occasional individuals with dark bronze new foliage or showy maroon markings on the foliage, and it is worthwhile growing plants from seed to make selections.

'Running Tapestry' is a selection from nature made by Jim Plyler of Natural Landscapes Nursery in eastern Pennsylvania. It's in the small size range, and has rounded leaves heavily marked with maroon. Var. *collina*, too, comes in a variety of forms, the best of which are just as handsome as the

Tiarella 'Martha Oliver' (Photo by Luc Klinkhamer)

newer hybrids, many of which have traits that are almost too exaggerated. 'Montrose Selection' is an especially good selection and has shallowly lobed leaves about 8–10cm (3½–4in) across with a small central maroon medallion, and a bronzish cast that lasts through spring. There are excellent pink flowers on dark stems to about 40cm (16in) high.

Special qualities: The wild forms of *T. cordifolia* have a simplicity of beauty much more suitable for naturalizing than that of the 'fancy foliage' cultivars. They also have vigour and hardiness that have been reduced in some of the new cultivars on the market.

Availability: In North America they are available from most nurseries that specialize in native plants. They are also available from specialist nurseries in Europe.

'Elizabeth Oliver'

Description: The frilly, deeply lobed, light green leaves are about 7cm (2¾in) across and marked with a central maroon blotch. The plants produce short runners 8–12cm (3½–4½in) long, and form a patch about 15cm (6in) high and 40cm (16in) wide. In spring there are scented pink flowers to 40cm (16in) high. This cultivar is named after our daughter, and was introduced by The Primrose Path in 1994.

Special qualities: This is one of the most delicate and pretty of the tiarella hybrids.

Availability: Can be found at many garden centres and mail-order nurseries.

Tiarella cordifolia var. *collina* at Green Spring Park, Virginia

Above *Tiarella* 'Green Sword' in seed
Right *Tiarella* 'Elizabeth Oliver'

'Green Sword'

Description – The leaves are deeply lobed and about 8cm (3½in) across, with a central maroon blotch and with the central lobe much extended, giving the leaf the shape of a broad sword. The foliage forms a clump about 20cm (8in) high and 30cm (12in) across. There are light pink flowers on 40cm (16in) stems in spring. It was introduced by The Primrose Path in 2000.

Special qualities: The unusual leaf shape does not occur in tiarella in nature, and is a good example of how hybridization can destabilize development to produce novel growth effects. In our garden 'Green Sword' has been the best performer of the tiarellas with extended leaf lobes.

Availability: *Tiarella* 'Green Sword' is available from a few mail-order nurseries or on the Internet.

Tiarella 'Pink Brushes'

'Martha Oliver'

Description: This cultivar has somewhat hairy, deeply cut leaves about 8cm (3½in) across, with light maroon markings that extend along the main veins of the lobes. The foliage makes a mound about 15cm (6in) high and 30cm (12in) wide. In spring there are white flowers to 40cm (16in) high. An early hybrid between *T. trifoliata* and *T. cordifolia*, this cultivar was selected at The Primrose Path and introduced in 1993.

Special qualities: 'Martha Oliver' forms a loose, spreading clump that will make a solid cover when planted in groups. The vibrant red winter foliage colour is the best of any tiarella we have seen.

Availability: *Tiarella* 'Martha Oliver' can be found at mail-order nurseries.

'Pink Brushes'

Description: 'Pink Brushes' has leaves lobed to about half way to the centre, and 10cm (4in) across. The foliage has a 'quilted' surface and light central maroon blotching. Plants form tight clumps about 25cm (10in) high and 35cm (14in) across. In spring there are pink flowers borne densely in spikes to 40cm (16in) high. This was a 2002 introduction from The Primrose Path.

Special qualities: This is an exceptionally vigorous and floriferous cultivar, and some of our plants have had well over 100 flower stems

Tiarella 'Pink Pearls'

in their second year in the garden. In addition the flowers are unusually long-lasting. In some of our tests 'Pink Brushes' grows well and makes thick clumps even where other tiarella cultivars do not thrive. It was exhibited by Blooms of Bressingham at the 2005 Chelsea Flower Show.

Availability: 'Pink Brushes' can be found at many mail-order nurseries in North America and will soon be available in Europe.

'Pink Pearls'

Description: This tiarella has rounded, entire, evenly green leaves 7–10cm (2¾–4in) across, and white flowers from pink buds in open panicles to about 40cm (16in) high. The inflorescences spread to the side and are branching like those of *T. trifoliata*. 'Pink Pearls' forms a clump of foliage that reaches about 20cm (8in) high and 35cm (14in) across. It is a hybrid between *T. cordifolia* var. *collina* 'George Schenk', a cultivar with unmarked foliage and pink flowers that flowers about two weeks later than other examples of *T. cordifolia* var. *collina*, and *T. trifoliata* var. *unifoliata*. The cross was made at The Primrose Path in 1994, and this cultivar introduced in 2002.

Special Qualities: 'Pink Pearls' was selected for its long flowering season, from late spring into July. Although its western parent, *T. trifoliata*, is only marginally winter-hardy in

Tiarella 'Running Tiger'

Tiarella 'Sea Foam'

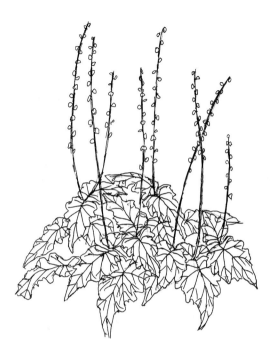

Pennsylvania, 'Pink Pearls' is fully hardy and is not affected by summer heat and humidity.
Availability: It can be obtained from many mail-order nurseries.

'Running Tiger'

Description: It has leaves somewhat similar to those of 'Pink Brushes' but with deeper lobing, and heavier and more irregular maroon blotching. The plants form clumps about 25cm (10in) high and 35cm across (14in), and in the second year they put out 40cm (16in) long runners. In mid-spring there are white flowers on 45cm (18in) long stems. 'Running Tiger' was a 2003 introduction from The Primrose Path.
Special qualities: This selection combines the clumping habit and heavy flowering of the large, non-running tiarellas with the ability to produce a moderate number of runners. It makes ground cover with more substance than the smaller stoloniferous forms.
Availability: It can be obtained from mail-order nurseries.

'Sea Foam'

Description: This is an especially vigorous selection recently introduced by Terra Nova. It has deeply cut leaves 8–10cm (3½–4in) across in a mound about 15cm (6in) high and 35cm (14in) wide. Each leaf is heavily marked with maroon, which extends out along the main veins. The white flowers are in very open panicles to about 40cm (16in) high.
Special qualities: We chose this for its very dramatic foliage and its vigour.
Availability: 'Sea Foam' is available at garden centres and mail-order nurseries.

Mitella

M. diphylla

Description: This species has heart-shaped foliage similar to that of *Tiarella c.* var. *cordifolia*. The leaves are even green and 6–8cm (3½in) across. Plants form a clump 15cm (6in) high by 25cm (10in) wide. In mid-spring there are white flowers like tiny snowflakes on narrow, erect 40cm (16in) stems.
Special qualities: A pretty spring wildflower, well worth growing.
Availability: It can be obtained from wildflower plant nurseries in North America and from a few specialists in the UK. Seed is available from society exchanges.

M. stylosa

Description: The leaves are sharp-lobed and longer than wide. They are about 4–5cm (1¾–2in) across and mottled with silvery grey-green, which is most prominent in winter. The foliage makes a dense mound only about 6cm (2½in) wide and 25cm (10in) across. In spring there are small, fringed red-purple flowers on narrow, 40cm (16in) long stems.
Special qualities: *M. stylosa* makes a very attractive little mound at the edge of a woodland bed. The flowers are interesting and unusual.
Availability: It can be obtained from a few specialist nurseries. Seed may be available from society exchanges.

Mitella diphylla

Mitella stylosa

4 Origins of the garden hybrids

There are many traits that contribute to making some forms of heuchera and related plants good garden plants, and others more interesting to a plant collector. These traits range from pleasing proportions, attractive foliage, and good flower size and colour to vigour and ease of cultivation. In general, each of the wild species offers at most only a few desirable traits, and it has been a challenge to the breeders to combine the best traits of many parents into new plants that are unlike anything that occurs in nature. Luckily, all the various species of heuchera and of tiarella are interfertile to some degree with each other within each genus. It is also very lucky that heuchera and tiarella can be crossed to make the sterile intergeneric hybrid *Heucherella*.

PROPORTIONS

In the wild species, overall plant size and density of foliage depend very much on the habitat. One of the large forest species of heuchera, *H. villosa* of the Upper South, has large, maple-shaped leaves that make a mound of loose foliage to 60cm (24in) across, with tiny whitish flowers on spreading wands to 90cm (3ft) high in summer. When *H. americana* grows in rich woods it can be quite large, with foliage over 30cm (12in) across and late spring flower stems to over 1m (3½ft) high, well above the foliage of surrounding plants. *H. richardsonii*, a prairie species, is also a large plant, and it needs to compete with other vigorous prairie species by getting its foliage and flowers up above the surrounding growth.

Many of the species that inhabit north-facing cliffs and rocky slopes have been important to horticulture. These plants tend to be more compact than those mentioned above, but are larger and less densely growing than the high montane types. *H. micrantha* of the North American Pacific Coast mountains inhabits cliffs, and makes attractive, loose foliage tufts about 30cm (12in) high in sheltered, moist crevices; the tiny flowers appear in diffuse sprays reaching 30cm (12in) or so above the leaves. *H. pulchella* of New Mexico and western Texas is a similarly sized species found in cliff crevices, while *H. sanguinea* is a taller plant growing in rock faces in Arizona. *H. grossulariifolia* and *H. cylindrica* are found on drier, more exposed western cliffs, and the foliage grows more compactly. The flowers are in cat's tail-shaped clusters at the ends of relatively long, 45–75cm (18–30in) long stems that reach out from the rock face so that pollinators can find them.

H. alba is the only eastern North American form showing the reduced proportions suitable to a montane habitat. This species grows among boulders in treeless sites above 1200m (3950ft) in a small area in eastern West Virginia and western Virginia. Wild plants are about 45cm (18in) tall when in flower, with relatively short, wide sprays of large flowers over full clumps of foliage across. The closely related *H. pubescens* is found on rocky slopes at lower altitudes, and is quite variable in size. Plants in heavily shaded sites may have very scanty foliage and flower stalks to 75cm (30in) high, but where there is more light the proportions are closer to those of *H. alba*.

The alpine heucheras such as the Rocky Mountain *H. parvifolia* var. *nivalis* and Californian *H. merriamii*, *H. hirsutissima*, and *H. elegans* grow as tightly compact tufts of small, overlapping leaves only 5cm (2in) high on slowly creeping woody stems among the rocks. *H. hallii* of the Colorado Rockies is a little larger, but is still a miniature species. Though the wild species are grown mostly by a small but devoted group of specialist rock gardeners, these alpines have contributed important qualities to the more widely grown garden hybrids.

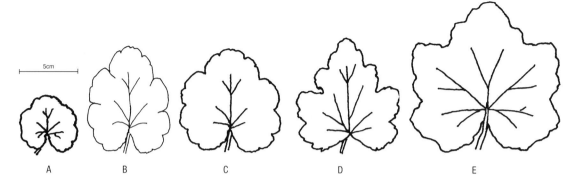

Variation in size and shape of leaves of wild heuchera and tiarella. Heuchera: **A.** *H. alpestris*, **B.** *H. cylindrica*, **C.** *H. sanguinea*, **D.** *H. pubescens*, **E.** *H. villosa*. Tiarella: **F.** *T. c.* var. *cordifolia*, **G.** *T. c.* var. *collina* lobed form, **H.** *T. trifoliata* var. *trifoliata*, **I.** *T. t.* f. *laciniata*, **J.** *T. t.* var. *unifoliata*.

Among the other genera, *Tiarella*, *Mitella* and *Tellima* are all forest plants that tolerate heavy shade. Eastern North American tiarellas and mitellas have showy flowers that open with the ephemeral spring flora in the sunlight of leafless deciduous forest; they are of the same proportions as mid-size heuchera. The western *Mitella pentandra* and *M. breweri* are skimpy little plants of open coniferous woods, and probably rely on pollinating flies to find their inconspicuous greenish flowers. We have seen *Tiarella trifoliata* growing in the Cascade Mountains in dense coniferous forest where there were few other herbaceous plants, and in full sun above the tree line in southern coastal Alaska. The plants in the two habitats differed very little in appearance. When in flower, *T. grandiflora* stands above the surrounding vegetation like a woodland heuchera.

To the general gardener, the most pleasing overall proportion for this group of plants is that the wands of flowers are about one and half to twice as tall as the basal foliage tuft is wide. The flowers should be large enough to have a significant presence, and to be held in a spray that is open enough to be airy but not so open as to look scanty or straggling. The leaves need to be on petioles of medium length, and dense enough for the foliage rosette to look full.

The older heuchera garden hybrids were derived largely from *H. sanguinea* and *H. americana* and, to a lesser extent, *H. cylindrica* and *H. richardsonii*. They are often tall and leggy in flower. Many other wild heucheras have better overall growth proportions, and *H. pulchella*, *H. hallii*, *H. elegans*, *H. micrantha*, and *H. alba* have provided the more pleasing proportions for the newer hybrids.

The eastern tiarellas have naturally pleasing proportions, but *T. trifoliata* has branching flower stems that reach out widely to the side. The early hybrids between the eastern and western tiarella types were selected for erect, well-proportioned flower stems, among other traits. *T.* 'Martha Oliver' and 'Elizabeth Oliver' have given their descendants, including the newer *Heucherella* and cut-leaf *Tiarella*, their good proportions.

FOLIAGE

The foliage of the heuchera group is probably the most variable of any group of garden perennials. Leaf size, shape, texture, coloration and foliage density are all factors that affect the appearance of the plants. In general, most of the foliage differences that are important to us occur between the species. However, many of the wild species in this group show genetic

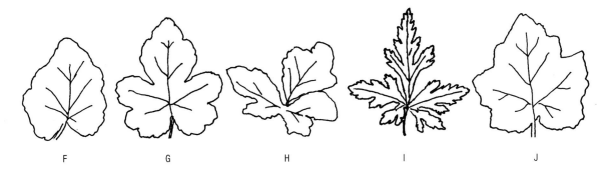

F   G   H   I   J

polymorphism for leaf shape and/or coloration in particular. In other words, in a given wild population of a single species, individuals may have different leaf shapes or coloration, and these differences are inherited in a simple way and have some adaptive value related, presumably, to differing environmental factors. As far as we know, there has been no breeding or selection done directly for leaf traits other than ruffling and coloration in heucheras, but in tiarellas the leaf shape has been one of the most important foliage considerations.

Leaf size may be as small as about 10mm (0.4in) across in the smallest of the alpine heuchera, to about 20cm (8in) across in the largest of the woodland types. As mentioned on page 8, this is an adaptation to environmental factors such as light levels and climatic stress. In cultivation, the leaf size is dependent on both the genetic make-up of the plant and soil fertility. Well-fed individuals of some cultivars may have leaves twice as wide as those grown in lean soil. The leaf size of tiarellas and the other small genera vary relatively little, in keeping with their smaller range of habitats.

Leaf shape varies greatly, too. Woodland heucheras like *H. villosa* and *H. americana* and the other large eastern North American shade species have five-lobed leaves shaped like those of maple trees. The leaves of most wild tiarellas, of *Tellima grandiflora*, and the relatively large *Mitella diphylla* are similar. Experiments have shown that tree leaves which are lobed like those of *Acer* (maple), *Platanus* (plane) or *Liriodendron* (tulip) assume a somewhat rolled, more streamlined shape in high winds and suffer less damage. This may also be true of the lobed leaves of heuchera and its relatives. Western North American heucheras from relatively dry sites have leaves that are smaller and oval. In some small heucheras (*H. parviflora* and *H. grossulariifolia*, for example) the leaves may have three distinct lobes, but there are no heucheras with leaf shapes that approach the very deep lobing and dissecting that occurs in forms of *Tiarella cordifolia* var. *collina* and, to a much greater degree, in *T. trifoliata*. In the latter the leaves may be actually compound, with each section highly divided in f. *laciniata*. The reasons for this leaf shape are not known, although compound leaf shape in woody plants is an adaptation to prevent ripping during storms.

In some of the maple-leafed heucheras (*H. villosa*, *H. micrantha* and *H. alba*) there is an occasional tendency for the leaf surface to become wavy. In *H. micrantha* this may be so pronounced as to be highly ruffled. Ruffling has the advantage of increasing the leaf surface available for photosynthesis without making the leaf any wider. Leaf ruffling does not seem to occur in the other genera.

There is a little variation in the texture of heuchera leaves, with the small montane species often having leaves that feel a little thicker and heavier textured. More pronounced is variation in pubescence.

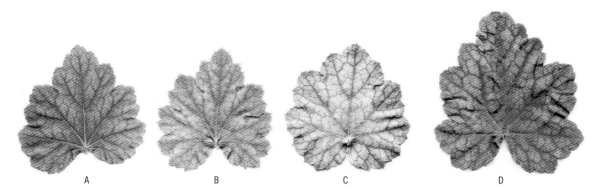

Silver patterning in parental species heuchera and its expression in selected hybrids derived from them:
A. *H. americana* Dale's Strain, **B.** *H. pubescens*, **C.** *H. pubescens* from Ice Mountain, West Virginia, **D.** Montrose Ruby, **E.** 'White Marble,' **F.** 'Regina' **G.** 'Silver Scrolls,' **H.** 'Silver Light'

H. richardsonii in the prairies and plains and *H. cylindrica* in the West, for example, have leaves, petioles and flower stalks that are noticeably hairy. *H. villosa* has fairly smooth leaves but furry petioles. Pubescent leaves probably have the function of reducing evaporation under dry, windy conditions; pubescent petioles may reduce damage from insect pests. The other genera do not vary enough to be important to us.

Leaf coloration in heucheras is the most important of the foliage considerations from a horticultural point of view. First, there is the background colour of the leaf. In the usual wild forms this is green during most of the growing season. In spring, however, it is common for the new foliage to emerge a bronzy or reddish-purple, as it does in many other plants from peonies to blackberries. This coloration supposedly protects the fast-growing tissues from harmful UV rays and/or helps to warm up the growing plant. We have also observed that in early summer the foliage of our non-hairy green-leafed heucheras in shady sites always has holes created by feeding slugs, whereas purple-leafed plants have almost no damage. The purple compounds of spring may help in some way to prevent pest damage to young foliage.

As the foliage of wild plants matures, so it gradually turns green. A slice through a maturing bronzy heuchera leaf will reveal under a magnifying glass or microscope that the tissues of the upper and lower halves of the leaf are sharply separate in coloration, with the lower side often remaining purple for some time even after the upper side has turned green. As autumn approaches the mature foliage will again become bronzy and stay that way through winter. We have not seen any western heucheras, except for *H. micrantha*, with distinct, seasonal foliage colour changes. Occasional wild forms of *H. villosa* and *H. micrantha* have been found that retain the early spring bronze coloration well into summer. In tiarellas, the upper side carries the bronze coloration, although this shows through the underside. In autumn, the eastern North American forms become purple-bronze to a variable degree. This is induced by light exposure as the patched appearance of the overlapping leaves shows. We have not seen seasonal purple coloration in the other genera.

In addition to the overall bronzing, the upper side of the leaf may be mottled with a pattern of different colours. In gardening books there seems to be no distinction made between natural colour patterning of leaves, and the variegation due to mutation ('sports'), with both being referred to as 'variegated'. Variegated sports are due to a chance loss of

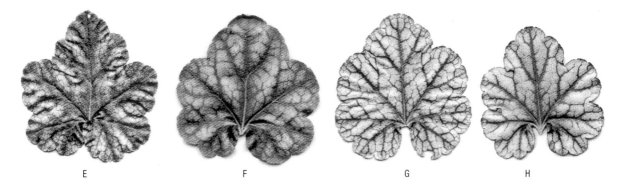

E   F   G   H

colour in part of the leaf. We use 'patterned' to refer to natural mottled coloration, and 'variegated' to refer to sports. In the latter, variegation is irregular and apparently random on the surface of the leaf, whereas patterning is regular and more or less symmetrical.

Heucheras and tiarellas often have dark maroon markings on the upper sides of the leaves. In heucheras, the pigment radiates from a patch at the base of the leaf out along the veins. Forms with this sort of leaf pattern are found primarily in the eastern spring-flowering species, although we have seen some expression of it in wild *H. micrantha*. Cultivars such as *H. americana* 'Garnet' are selections with very well developed maroon leaf markings. In tiarellas, the eastern types often have maroon leaf markings. They usually consist of a central blotch at the base of the leaf with irregularly shaped extensions or archipelagos of colour out along the veins. *T. polyphylla* of eastern Asia and at least one Asian *Mitella* also have a maroon pigment that follows the veins of the upper side of the leaf.

In heucheras and eastern North American tiarellas, the maroon leaf markings seem to be brought about by development of the leaves during cool temperatures. The markings fade in heucheras as summer comes, but seem to be more or less stable in the leaves in tiarellas. In some forms the first leaves in spring are heavily marked and later leaves are almost unmarked. And we have tried interesting wholesale producers in our tiarella cultivars with

handsome maroon-marked foliage, only to have our propagated stock, grown through winter in heated greenhouses, come to maturation with unmarked green leaves. Conversely, photographs of tiarellas used for advertising may show plants purposely grown under conditions that exaggerate the leaf markings which occur in the average garden. (It's also worth adding that similar maroon leaf markings are found in many other plants, including *Polygonum* (knotweed), trillium, hepatica, corydalis, *Cardamine* (toothwort), white clover and *Corylus* (hazelnut). The dark pigment may help to warm up the leaf tissues in cool weather.)

Another very conspicuous part of leaf patterning is the silver-grey or white leaf marbling of some forms. This, too, occurs only on the upper side of the leaves and, unlike the dark coloration discussed above, is due to leaf structure rather than pigmentation. The cuticle is raised above the underlying tissues between the leaf veins to make a reflective open space, as can be demonstrated by running your fingernail across a silvered leaf. The trait varies from small, barely visible patches to virtually the whole leaf surface. Wild forms of heuchera with this feature occur mainly in the eastern North American, spring-flowering species.

H. americana Dale's Strain is a seed-strain selected for prominent silver marbling. *H. pubescens* often has marbled leaves, and some plants we saw growing wild at Ice Mountain, West Virginia, were totally white

Heuchera micrantha with maroon vein pigment in Santa Barbara Botanic Garden, California (Photo by Kary Arimoto-Mercer)

with a tracing of green veins. *H. longiflora*, a species found on limestone ledges in the southern Appalachians, also has nicely marbled leaves, but it hasn't been used in breeding at all. Silver marbling has not been found in tiarella, but a marbled selection has been made from the wild *Tellima grandiflora* ('Forest Frost'), and the Asian *Mitella stylosa* has indistinct marbling. The appearance of light marbling is affected by variation in the appearance of the cuticle itself, which may have a matt finish or be shiny. A shiny cuticle on highly marbled leaves can give a very decorative metallic sheen to foliage. We have seen no explanation of the function of light marbling in the life of the plant, but it occurs in many families unrelated to heuchera.

In our garden, herbaceous plants such as *Asarum* (wild ginger), cyclamen, *Viola* (violet), hepatica, *Pulmonaria* (lungwort) and *Hydrophyllum* (waterleaf) all show similar leaf coloration, and there are many other examples

to be found. All these plants have a common growth habit (relatively low and usually clumping) and a preference for shade, but the woody vines *Schizophragma hydrangeoides* 'Moonlight' and *Clematis terniflora* also have light marbling on their leaves.

Robbin Moran (2004) has discussed frond structure in tropical rain forest ferns that grow under low light conditions. The surfaces of the upper epidermis cells of these plants are convex, and focus light down on to the chloroplasts. The plants have an iridescent blue-green sheen, which seems to mean that they are also able to absorb more of the desirable red part of the light. We think that the air spaces in marbled leaves may have some sort of analogous role. Perhaps they focus more light to the chloroplasts, or reflect harmful ultraviolet while acting as mini-greenhouses to warm tissues in the spring, or they may facilitate gas exchange and cell respiration.

Occasional individual tiarellas of the eastern forms have a noticeable pattern of lighter green mottling similar to the silver marbling of heucheras. We cannot detect any structural differences in the darker and lighter areas of the leaves, and assume that this is simply a difference in the pigmentation.

FLOWER FORM AND COLOUR

Wild heuchera flowers vary greatly in size and shape. We have discussed the basic morphology in Chapter 1. At one end of the flower size range are species such as *H. americana* and *H. parvifolia*, especially *H. parvifolia* var. *nivalis*, and their flowers are reduced to little more than the sexual parts; they are green or purplish-green, and only a couple of millimetres across. *H. americana* presents its flowers at the tops of long – often 1m (3½ft) or more – stems above surrounding woodland vegetation, while *H. parvifolia* var. *nivalis* bears its flowers on 15–25cm (6–10in) long stems among alpine rocks. Both are probably attracting small flies as pollinators. *H. micrantha* and *H. villosa* have tiny bells about 3mm (0.1in) long, with projecting stamens and styles, and are borne on 30–90cm (12–36in) long stems in airy sprays like baby's-breath. They are probably for pollinating by flies or small bees.

In western North America there are a number of species with pink, red, or white tubular flowers 6–8mm (0.2–0.3in) long, arranged facing outwards on the flower stalks; a few types are sweet-smelling and are designed to attract bees, butterflies, moths and hummingbirds. They also attract gardeners. Less well known are two eastern species with the largest flowers of all: *H. pubescens* and *H. alba*, both inhabitants of the Appalachians. The flowers of these two species are wide bells up to about 7mm (0.3in) wide and 10mm (0.4in) long. *H. pubescens*, which inhabits shaded rocky slopes, has green flowers often marked with purple in an open spray about 60cm (24in) tall and is probably attracting flies and bees. *H. alba* grows on mountain tops in sun, and has greenish-white to cream-coloured flowers in shorter, denser sprays, with each flower tending to be held in a more hanging position. This may be an adaptation to pollination by bumblebees, which are so heavy that they need to hang from flowers in order to feed.

Generally the flower stems of heucheras are green, matching the petioles. In some species, such as *H. cylindrica* and *H. alba*, various individuals have more or less contrasting reddish coloration that extends from the base of the inflorescence up through the pedicels of the whole flower panicle.

Wild tiarellas vary in flower colour, size, and substance, the density of the flower panicle, the number of panicles per inflorescence, the number of inflorescences per plant, and the height and angle of the flower stems. Running forms of *T. cordifolia* have stems of flowers to about 30cm (12in) high scattered as single erect spikes over a mat of foliage. The flowers are in relatively sparse panicles, and are white or appear very light pink because of pale red-purple colouration of the sepals. The clump-forming *T. cordifolia* var. *collina*, on the other hand, has 20 or more erect stems of flowers to 40cm (16in) above each plant. The flowers are sometimes scented and tend to have broader petals and sepals, and to be denser in the panicle. Some forms have more intensely red-purple sepals, so that white or light pink flowers open from pink buds. In addition, the flower stems may be contrasting dark purplish rather than the usual green. All this, in addition to the foliage traits discussed earlier, gives a very showy and pleasing display. The western North American tiarellas are less showy and richly coloured, with sparser panicles of less substantial white flowers on spreading, often branched stems. Probably the showier tiarellas are pollinated more often by bees, and the less showy by flies.

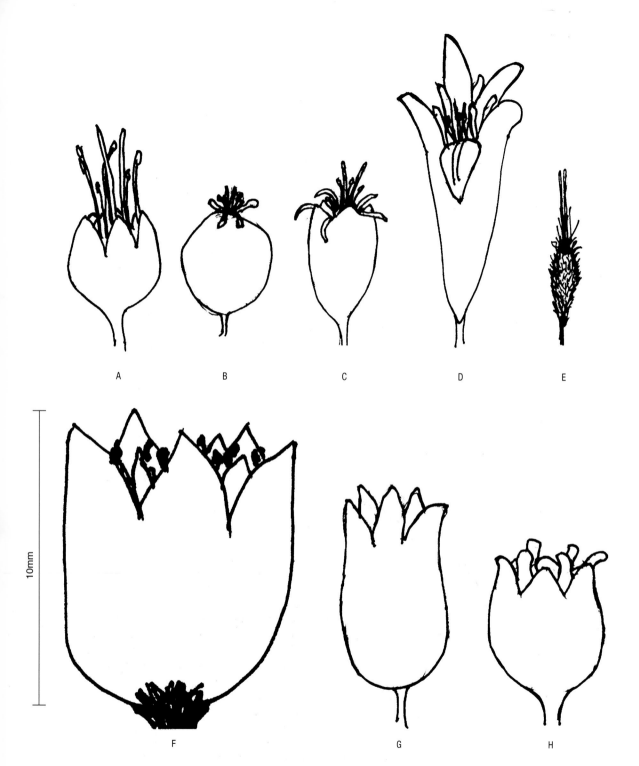

Heuchera species flower diversity in size and shape:
A. *H. americana*, **B.** *H. merriamii*, **C.** *H. pulchella*, **D.** *H. sanguinea*,
E. *H. villosa*, **F.** *H. pubescens*, **G.** *H. cylindrica*, **H.** *H. hallii*

VIGOUR

The vigour of wild species can be discussed only in terms of growth under cultivation, since we can assume it is nearly perfect under natural conditions or the wild species would not have survived. In cultivation, the vigour of these species depends on how close the garden conditions are to those in the wild. Climate is the most important factor, and generally the lowland species succeed best in the gardens of most of North America and Europe. Alpine heucheras are surprisingly adaptable, but do not last very long in south-eastern North America; some Pacific coast species, such as *H. micrantha*, are not hardy in the cold winters of the north-eastern states. The north-western wild tiarellas are not happy in the hot, humid summers and the cold winters of the northeastern US and south-eastern Canada. Part of breeding satisfactory garden plants from this group has been selecting hybrids with the vigour of those species most suited to cultivation.

COMBINATION OF TRAITS

Many of the traits that we have discussed seem to be inherited in a very simple manner, many probably depending on single genes or very small numbers of genes. The effect of this is that when crosses are made between different forms, the traits of the offspring tend to be like one parent or the other rather than a smooth blend between them. Leaf background colour is either green or purple, for example. Other traits, like flower size or plant height, are less clear cut, but when groups of sibling seedlings of mixed parentage are examined, there will always be great diversity of size, growth habit and coloration, rather than homogeneity. In addition, some similar traits in different species don't seem to be due to the effects of exactly the same genes. For example, some very small alpine heucheras seem to be using different genes to achieve a dwarfing effect. When the species are hybridized, some of the offspring will be smaller than the parents, some larger. This effect is seen also in tiarellas, with some offspring of crosses between the eastern and western types, both with deeply lobed leaves, having leaves that are even more dissected than those of either parental type.

Similarly, there have been different ways for wild species to adapt their metabolisms to suit their environments. These involve, for example, genes that promote embryo growth or seed germination under specialized conditions, or that enhance photosynthesis, cold tolerance or drought-resistance, and over the millennia a number of different solutions to the same problems have evolved. Again, though, relatively few genes are involved, and when hybrids are made between species there is great diversity in a sibling group in the seed set, germination success and seedling vigour.

Some species are much more compatible with each other as parents than others. Generally, this is directly related to how closely related are the parents. *Heuchera americana* and *H. pubescens*, and *H. americana* and *H. richardsonii* produce such vigorous hybrids together that hybrids are common in nature where the plants share the same geographic range. *H. villosa* and *H. americana*, on the other hand, are much less closely related and do not hybridize in nature. If crosses are made, much of the hybrid seed does not germinate, but some of the hybrid plants that do grow will have high garden vigour. Reduction of compatibility between the parental types is not really caused by overall genetic difference as such, but by crucial differences in a few genes that control the metabolic pathways that are necessary for successful germination and growth.

It is still possible, but less likely, that a successful match of genes will occur in the hybrid seed. In the heuchera group evolution has involved little change in the structure or number of the chromosomes, even between closely related genera, like *Heuchera* and *Tiarella*. As a result, there is not much of a mechanical genetic barrier to hybridization attempted by the breeder. Maintenance of separate species in nature must depend on the use of different pollinators and separation in range, habitat and flowering time. Nevertheless, it seems quite surprising that tiny alpine and large woodland heuchera can produce normally growing hybrids together.

In fact hybridization in heuchera and closely related genera is successful to an extent that is unusual compared to other plant genera popular in horticulture. In phlox, for example, only combinations between certain species groups produce viable seed, and almost all the hybrid plants are sterile. Primulas are generally similar, with only a few combinations – for example among the Vernales group which includes *P. vulgaris*, *P. veris*, *P. juliae* and *P. elatior* – yielding hybrids viable and fertile enough to give breeding lines. Hostas and hemerocallis are perhaps the closest equivalent genera in crossability of species, although they do not have the diversity of form found in heuchera.

It is ironic that in heucheras the colourful foliage available for breeding work has come mainly from *H. americana* and *H. villosa*, two of the species with the smallest flowers, whereas showy flowers have come from North American species with nearly plain green leaves. This has caused the garden hybrids to be grown either for foliage or flowers, but not both.

One peculiarity in the combining of traits has been very important in heuchera breeding. This is the relationship between foliage and flower colour. Since dark purple foliage goes with dark-coloured flower stems, one would guess that plants with dark purple foliage would be more likely to have dark pink or red flowers. On the contrary, individual plants with purple foliage almost always have white or pale pink flowers. Plants with good rose-red flowers have had at best light bronze foliage, and no plants with clear red flowers and dark purple foliage have yet come on to the market, despite advertising claims. The genetic basis of this problem is unknown.

Heucherella 'Quicksilver' flower

Heucheras and tiarellas are much more different and are not known to hybridize in nature, but even they can produce hybrid seedlings if cross-pollinated. Most of the seed does not germinate, and most of the seedlings that do grow are stunted. By chance a few hybrids, however, are vigorous enough in cultivation to have become good garden plants. They generally resemble tiarellas more than heucheras in overall appearance and growth habit: the flowers are intermediate in shape, resembling a dish rather than a bell; the leaves may be as deeply lobed as those of the more extreme tiarella; the red-purple or purple-bronze foliage coloration of a heuchera is inherited as chocolate-bronze; and there may be full expression of heuchera-style silver patterning, combined with a central maroon patch.

The importance of all this to the breeder is that if he makes enough crosses and raises enough seedlings, the law of averages will be on his side. Even though most of the plants he raises will be mediocre and some will be nearly inviable, there will also be a few where all the good traits come together to superb effect.

5 History and discussion: breeding heucheras, tiarellas and heucherellas

HEUCHERA

The beginning

Heuchera first reached Europe in the 1600s, when *H. americana* was sent from the American colonies. It was well known to the Native Americans as a medicinal plant and called alum root by the colonists. The roots were used as a poultice on wounds, and had the effect of pulling injured tissues together as would alum. *H. americana* was described by Linnaeus in 1753 in the first edition of *Species Plantarum*, and the genus was named after his correspondent Johann von Heucher (1667–1747), a physician and professor in Wittenberg and later in Dresden. By the 1800s other species, such as *H. richardsonii*, *H. cylindrica*, *H. villosa* and *H. sanguinea*, were being grown in Europe, but it was not until the French nurseryman Emile Lemoine crossed *H. sanguinea* with *H. americana* in the 1890s that horticultural hybrid combinations were made.

In those days it was common to use Latin-style names for plant selections, and one of the hybrids was named 'Brizoides'. In the years since, this name – often given as *H.* x *brizoides* – has been applied to a whole class of heuchera hybrids that resemble *H. sanguinea* (the Bressingham hybrids, for example), and so we use the name Brizoides in this way rather than with the single quotes that denote a cultivar. Later selections of Brizoides were made that combined the flower size and coloration of *H. sanguinea* with the leaf coloration of *H. americana*, and

Heuchera sanguinea var. *pulchra*

Santa Barbara Botanic Garden headquarters with *Heuchera* 'Susanna' (Photo by Kary Arimoto-Mercer)

these were widely sold. Later, *H. micrantha* was crossed into *H.* Brizoides to make the flower panicles more open and airy.

The Bloom family in England grew *H.* Brizoides for the cut-flower market in the 1920s. The late Alan Bloom made many crosses within *H.* Brizoides and back to *H. sanguinea*, and introduced many excellent selections over an extraordinarily long career. Almost all were refinements on the basic combination of colourful flowers from *H. sanguinea*, with silvery marbling and often dark veining from *H. americana*, although some crosses were made with *H. cylindrica*. The latter input had the effect of producing flower panicles that were more in a cat's tail or poker shape on relatively long, erect stems. Many of the Blooms selections are widely available today.

At about the same time as the first heuchera hybrids were becoming well known in Europe, a taxonomic authority on the genus,

C O Rosendahl, at the University of Minnesota, was experimenting with another group of hybrids. They were from crosses made in 1914 between *H. sanguinea* and *H. richardsonii*. Rosendahl remarked on the wide diversity of forms among the hybrids, and mentions that many plants were still growing in the University of Minnesota garden in 1936 (Rosendahl et al, 1936). Rosendahl's accompanying photograph shows these to be large plants, similar to a series of hybrids that we made involving *H. richardsonii* in the late 1990s. Rosendahl was surprised at how vigorous and successful these hybrids were.

Rancho Santa Ana and Canyon hybrids

By the 1950s, Lee Lenz at the Rancho Santa Ana Botanic Garden in Claremont, California, became interested in hybridizing the native *H. maxima*, a large species from the Santa Barbara Channel Islands, with *H. sanguinea* to develop new garden hybrids for southern California. Although the flowers of *H. maxima* are small and greenish-white, it is attractive and imposing because of its large, full inflorescences that arch from a clump of hairy, plain green leaves (page 24). The use of white, pink, and red flowered *H. sanguinea* parents resulted in hybrids 60–80cm (24–31in) tall, with inflorescences more erect than those of *H. maxima*. The flowers are only medium-sized, being 5–6mm (0.19–0.2in) long, and mostly urn-shaped, but the selections made, such as 'Santa Ana Cardinal', Wendy' and 'Susanna', have clear colours and are impressive and beautiful in the massed plantings that can be seen at the botanic garden. *H. maxima* is also very drought-resistant, and its hybrid progeny can be grown in southern California without summer watering. On the negative side, this group of heuchera is hardy only to about -10°C (14°F), and are not suitable for outside gardening in much of North America.

At the Santa Barbara Botanic Garden in the 1980s, Dara Emery used *H. elegans*, *H. hirsutissima* and *H. pringlei* (now included in *H. merriamii*), all heucheras from the mountains of California, with *H. sanguinea*-form garden hybrids to create the Canyon hybrids that are small to medium size, showy plants suitable for rock garden and containers. The California wild parents inhabit rocky sites, and grow as spreading mats of foliage rosettes bearing white to pink flowers on 15–30cm (6–12in) long stems in spring. The prettiest forms have flowers with pink calyces and relatively large projecting white petals, making a frilly, foamy effect *en masse*. Most of the Canyon hybrids are intermediate in size between the parental types, with the intense flower colour of *H. sanguinea*. This series of hybrids is still not widely known outside California.

Origin of purple and silver foliage

H. 'Palace Purple' arrived on the horticultural scene in the early 1980s. Everyone seems to agree that it was grown from seed sent to Kew Gardens from an Edgar Wherry collection, but there has been confusion about its real identity. It was introduced as a purple-leafed form of *H. micrantha* var. *diversifolia*. Wherry spent a lot of time in the field in the southeastern states, and had a special interest in heuchera and tiarella. It is likely that he would have collected the purple form of *H. villosa* that occurs occasionally in the southern Appalachians, and 'Palace Purple' is indistinguishable from this form. Specific traits such as spiny seeds and winter hardiness in cold climates indicate that 'Palace Purple' is an *H. villosa* form, and similar forms of *H. villosa* f. *purpurea* were being grown by members of the American Rock Garden Society before the advent of 'Palace Purple'. We think it is possible that '*Heuchera macrorhiza*' (a synonym of *H. villosa*) was written on the seed envelope, but was misread as *Heuchera micrantha*.

'Palace Purple' became very popular with the general gardening public, and made gardeners and nursery professionals much more aware of heuchera as foliage plants. Unfortunately many of the plants propagated under this name were raised from seed, and the quality of the resulting strain has become very uneven. At the present time, mediocre seed strain forms are much overused in landscaping.

A second heuchera foliage selection became widely available in the 1980s. This was *H. americana* Dale's Strain, based on a selection from the southern Appalachians that had especially well-silvered foliage. Dale Hendricks has continued to propagate this strain at North Creek Nursery in eastern Pennsylvania. Nancy Goodwin at Montrose Nursery in North Carolina grew 'Palace Purple' and Dale's Strain together in her garden, and in the late 1980s found that a lot of seed that she had planted had produced a group of obvious hybrid seedlings. Some were later sold under the name Montrose Ruby, the name referring to a group of similar plants rather than a single cultivar.

The individual that we bought from Montrose resembles *H. americana* more than 'Palace Purple'. The foliage is relatively smooth rather than hairy, and the leaves are silvered about as much as the best of the Dale's Strain forms. The background colour is rich, clear burgundy, much better than the brownish purple colour of 'Palace Purple', and the purple and silver complement each other beautifully. The plant has been exceptionally vigorous. On the other hand, the foliage mound is open and a bit sparse, and the creamy white, tiny flowers are on long, gawky stems like those of *H. americana*. A couple of selected plants of Montrose Ruby became the breeding starting point of all the purple and silver hybrids on the market today. The coloration and vigour have allowed us to explore all sorts of hybrid combinations, but improving the proportions and flower size has been a continuing challenge.

At The Primrose Path we became interested in native heucheras by the early 1980s, growing from seed local western Pennsylvanian *H. americana*, and *H. pubescens* from the West Virginia shale barrens. We selected plants of *H. pubescens* with especially prominent and attractive silver marbling, and kept them in a bed with an individual of *H.* White Cloud, a white-flowered *H.* Brizoides strain. Seed from the selected *H. pubescens* produced a number of hybrids with White Cloud in the late 1980s. The best was chosen on the basis of well-marbled foliage and large white flowers, and was introduced as 'White Marble' in our 1995 catalogue. It has flowers that are narrower than the tubby bells of *H. pubescens*, but wider than those of White Cloud and about as long as any of the Brizoides at 9–10mm (0.35–0.4in). They are borne in full 60cm (24in) long sprays similar to those of *H. pubescens*. 'White Marble' is a very vigorous and well-proportioned plant, and it gave us the idea that there was much potential for heuchera hybrids involving new combinations of species and cultivars.

One obvious combination was 'White Marble' and Montrose Ruby, and a cross in 1992 produced a group of hybrids of which the most outstanding was named 'Quilters' Joy' (introduced by us in 1997), the name referring to the crisply patterned silver and purple foliage. It was widely distributed by Terra Nova Nurseries under the incorrect name 'Checkers', and is still found on wholesale lists under that name. The silver leaf patterning of 'Quilters' Joy', coming from both *H. americana* and *H. pubescens*, covers the whole leaf surface between the veins which are dark and contrasting. The leaves are angular like those of Montrose Ruby, but relatively small at about 7cm (2¾in) wide. The flowers are white and attractive, although smaller than those of White Cloud, showing the persistence of influence of *H. americana* genes on flower size. However, the inflorescence is erect and well proportioned to about 60–70cm (24–27in) high.

The next spring (in 1993) we crossed 'Quilters' Joy' with a vigorous pink-flowered *H.* Brizoides cultivar, 'Chatterbox'. This popular variety has well-silvered green foliage, and medium-sized (in relation to other Brizoides) flowers on 60–80cm (24–31in) long stems. The best of the progeny was 'Regina', named after our associate Regina Birchem and introduced in 1997. This selection has leaves that are larger, being about 10cm (4in) across and more rounded than those of 'Quilters' Joy', with the silver patterning a little more metallic. The flowers are similar to those of 'Chatterbox', appearing on stems up to 80cm (31in) high.

When flowering in shade, 'Regina' can be a little floppier than we like but it is still one of our favourites. It is the first of the complex heuchera hybrids to combine all the basic traits that we consider highly desirable into a single plant: the silver leaf patterning comes from *H. pubescens* and *H. americana*, the purple leaf coloration from *H. villosa*, the large flowers from *H. pubescens* and *H. sanguinea*, and their colour from *H. sanguinea*. A back-

Heuchera 'White Marble'

cross to *H.* 'Quilters' Joy' produced the selection 'Harmonic Convergence' with larger pink flowers in better proportioned inflorescences, and purple and silver leaves.

Another breeding line at The Primrose Path began with two species of western North American montane heuchera: *H. pulchella*, from the cliffs of New Mexico and western Texas, and *H. hallii*, from the Pikes Peak region of Colorado. These are small species with tufts of unmarked green foliage and fairly showy flowers to 20cm (8in) high for *H. hallii*, and 30cm (12in) for *H. pulchella*. The two were combined into the SanPico hybrids which had pale pink to white flowers. The inflorescence height varied from about 15cm–30cm (6in–12in), indicating that the two parental species have differences in the genetic control of height, and that dwarfing can be somewhat additive.

Heuchera 'Harmonic Convergence'

Heuchera hallii

One of the most attractive of these hybrids, *H.* 'SanPico Rosita', a 15cm (6in) tall plant with good pale pink flowers from dark pink buds, was crossed with *H.* 'Regina' in 1994, and a very variable group of progeny was the result. A set of six plants was selected, named the 'Petite Series', and introduced by us in 1997. Three of them have bronze and silver foliage, and light pink flowers: 'Petite Pearl Fairy' to 30cm (12in) high; 'Petite Marbled Burgundy' to 40cm (16in) high and 'Petite Ruby Frills' to 30cm (12in) high. 'Petite Lime Sherbet' and 'Petite Pink Bouquet' have green leaves marked with silver, and medium pink flowers to 30cm (12in) high. 'Petite Bronze

Pearl', with light bronze leaves and white flowers to 40cm (16in) high, was later dropped from our catalogue, but was an important parent for further breeding work.

We also explored using *H. cylindrica* as a wild parent. We chose an especially large-flowered individual of the short-stemmed *H. cylindrica* var. *alpina* from a group we had grown from wild seed, and crossed it with *H.* Brizoides 'Chatterbox', a cultivar with fairly large, 6mm (0.2in) long pink flowers, and silver patterning on the leaves. The best selection from the hybrid progeny was 'Coral Bouquet', a plant with lightly silver-patterned leaves and very large coral pink flowers in a

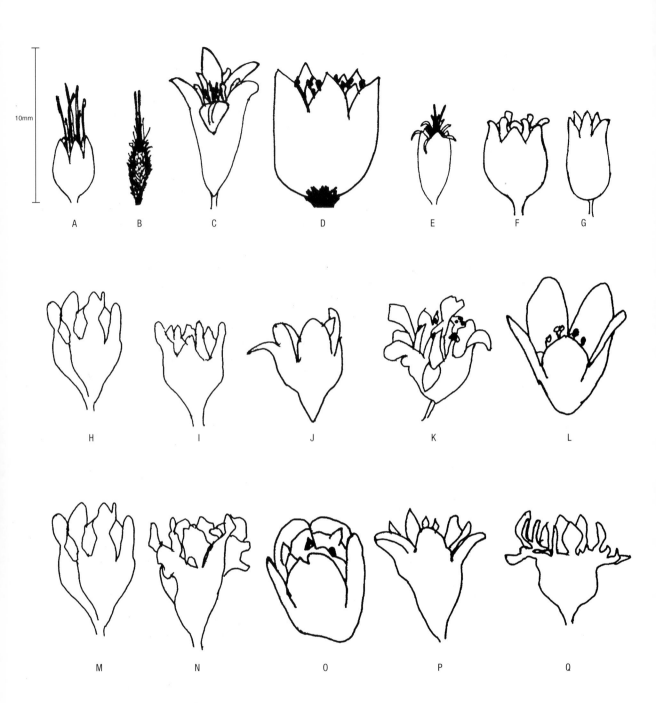

Progression in heuchera flower size and shape in the breeding programme at The Primrose Path.
A. *H. americana*, **B.** *H. villosa*, **C.** *H. sanguinea*, **D.** *H. pubescens*, **E.** *H. pulchella*, **F.** *H. hallii*,
G. *H. cylindrica*, **H.** 'White Marble,' **I.** 'Regina,' **J.** 'Silver Scrolls,' **K.** 'Petite Marbled Burgundy,'
L. 'Coral Bouquet,' **M.** 'Moonlight,' **N–Q.** 2005 unnamed selections.

loose cat's tail-shaped panicle on stems to about 45cm (18in) high. This, we think, has the showiest flowers of any heuchera, but it has not come into great popularity, probably because the green foliage is a marketing liability and because it requires excellent winter drainage.

'Petite Bronze Pearl' was crossed with 'Harmonic Convergence' in 1996 with very good results. As a result, four plants, a record, were selected for introduction. These Silver hybrids had highly silvered foliage and erect stems of white or pink flowers. 'Silver Scrolls' has proven the most popular of the group. It has rounded leaves with a very dark tracery of veins, and metallic silver between the veins above and dark red-purple below. The white flowers are small by today's standards, but are an attractive presence in tight panicles to about 60cm (24in) high. 'Silver Lode' is somewhat similar, with matt silver leaves and slightly taller inflorescences. 'Raspberry Ice' has highly silvered, more angular leaves and larger pink flowers on shorter stems. 'Silver Maps' is a smaller, very silvery form with white flowers.

Our next project was to combine the foliage of this group of well-silvered forms with our selected *H. villosa* f. *purpurea* 'Bronze Wave'. The *H. villosa* forms are among the most vigorous and enduring heucheras for growing in eastern North America (see page 27), and 'Bronze Wave' is an exceptionally attractive form. We planted out many hundreds of seedlings, most of which resembled the *H. villosa* parent much more than the silver hybrids. In the end we introduced the one plant that we had selected for vigour and colour directly from the seed tray! 'Frosted Violet' has 'Silver Lode' as the silver parent, and has leaves of the *H. villosa* shape, patterned with an unusual silvery violet colour. The small pink flowers are similar in shape to those of *H. villosa*, and appear in late spring, lasting through the summer. This has proven to be our second most popular plant.

Although we had grown *H. pubescens* for many years and used it as a foundation stone

of our early heuchera breeding programme, it was only in the late 1990s that we grew *H. alba*. Our seed was from Green Spring Park in Fairfax County, Virginia, from stock from the summit of Spruce Knob, West Virginia. In Elizabeth Wells' 1984 paper, she lumps *H. alba* in with the normal range of variation of *H. pubescens*, so we had not made a special effort to obtain this form. In fact the plants that we grew from this seed were very different from our *H. pubescens*, with larger flowers, often of a creamy white colour and shorter, denser inflorescences. In the spring of 1999, our breeding focus shifted to an emphasis on developing plants with larger flowers of clear colour and pleasing shape on well-proportioned inflorescences.

In the first round of crosses we combined *H. alba* with some of our hybrid selections, large and small. A couple of the offspring were remarkable in their size and vigour. 'Shenandoah Mountain', a 'Silver Scrolls' x *H. alba* hybrid, was introduced on the basis of its unusual size and habit. It has leafy flower stems to 80cm (31in) high and medium-sized, creamy white flowers over bronze and silver foliage. 'Purple Mountain Majesty', a cross between an unnamed miniature selection and *H. alba*, has white flowers that are as large as those of *H. alba* and almost globular on very erect, 40cm (16in) stems over purple foliage, while 'Moonlight' has equally large pale green flowers on 40cm (16in) long erect stems, over contrasting silver and purple foliage.

Other selections have very good flower traits but are lacking in other ways, and have been used as parents for further breeding, but not introduced. Crosses to our large flowered selection 'Coral Bouquet' and back-crosses to our best *H. alba* individuals followed, and then crosses among the best offspring. In the spring of 2005 we had a large and varied group of seedlings flowering for the first time and, as we write, are selecting individuals with the largest flowers we have seen in a heuchera, with shapes that vary from almost globular to nearly saucer-like. The figure on page 126

sums up the progression in flower size and shape that has taken place in our breeding programme.

Over the years we have struggled with the problems of flower size and foliage-flower colour, as mentioned in Chapter 4. The basic stock of purple-leafed cultivars is so founded on species with tiny flowers that it has taken repeated crossing and back-crossing to the largest-flowered species to get the hybrid flower size we wanted. We have selected for intense pinks, but have yet to introduce a dark purple-leafed plant with flowers of the intense dark pink or red we have been aiming at.

Breeding at Terra Nova

Dan Heims at Terra Nova Nurseries in Portland, Oregon became especially attracted to heucheras when, in the late 1980s, he found a variegated plant at a retail nursery and introduced it as 'Snow Storm'. He purchased *H.* Montrose Ruby from Nancy Goodwin, harvested seed from crosses between these plants and *H. americana*, and started over 10,000 seedlings for evaluation. 'Pewter Veil', which has a more metallic finish to the leaves than Montrose Ruby and an inflorescence more like that of *H. americana*, was introduced in 1992. More combinations of this type (the Veil Series) were soon selected and introduced. Most are fairly similar, and differ chiefly in the red-purple foliage hue, the amount of silvering on the leaves and crispness of the patterning, and the presence or absence of a metallic sheen on the upper side of the leaves. They have been marketed as foliage plants only because they bear tall stems of very small greenish or whitish flowers.

Heims then brought into the mix a form of *H. micrantha* with very ruffled leaves, and combined it with the Veil series to produce a series of variants with ruffled, red-purple foliage. The flowers of *H. micrantha* are tiny and greenish-white; combining them with those derived from *H. americana* and *H. villosa* did nothing to increase the flower

size or colour. In addition, the relative lack of hardiness of *H. micrantha* has persisted in the ruffled hybrids and makes some of them unreliable over winter in the colder parts of the Midwest and eastern North America. Bringing plants of the *H. sanguinea* type into this group of hybrids has increased the flower size somewhat, and improved flower colour greatly in cultivars such as 'Fireworks', 'Smokey Rose' and 'Vesuvius.' Recently Terra Nova has tried inducing polyploidy, and one result has been the introduction of 'Chinook', a tetraploid version of 'Fireworks' with relatively large flowers. Terra Nova has also worked with *H. cylindrica* hybrids to produce plants suitable for the cut-flower market. One selection, 'Florist's Choice', has flower stems to about 90cm (3ft) long and red flowers in a tight, cat's tail-shaped spike.

Sports have continued to play a large role in the Terra Nova programme. Since their plants are propagated in large numbers by tissue culture, the chances are good for occasional foliage mutations appearing in their stock (page 146). Many of these mutations have been of the chimaera type, familiar to the gardener in the form of variegated hostas with patches of differently coloured leaf tissue ('Mardi Gras' and 'Peachy Keen', for example), but recently they have introduced whole-plant somatic mutations with abnormal pigmentation. 'Amber Waves', introduced in 2000, is derived from a ruffled, red-purple form that appears to have lost both purple and green pigmentation on the upper leaf surface. The foliage of 'Amber Waves' is yellowish-tan on the upper side and red-purple below. Unlike leaf variegation, this mutation is heritable (i.e., it breeds 'true'), and other pigment-deficient cultivars have been bred from 'Amber Waves'. *H.* 'Lime Rickey' and the closely similar '*H.* 'Key Lime Pie', are green forms that lack part of the ability to make chlorophyll, and are pale yellow-green. Because much of the pigment used to manufacture food is missing in these plants, they are far less vigorous than their

Heuchera micrantha 'Ruffles'

normal counterparts. The descendant 'Marmalade' resembles 'Amber Waves', and was introduced as a more vigorous alternative.

The Morden Research Station

Beginning in the late 1970s, H H Marshall and later Lynn Collicutt at the Morden Research Station near Brandon, Manitoba, crossed *H. richardsonii* with *H.* Brizoides types to produce a series of very hardy heucheras for Canadian gardeners. The resulting introductions, such as 'Brandon Pink', 'Brandon Glow' and 'Northern Fire', resemble Brizoides and can be used in a similar way in the garden, but they have inherited the hardiness of *H. richardsonii*.

Other breeders

Many others have introduced cultivars of heuchera. In general they have been nurseries and gardeners who have found interesting seedlings among their stock, rather than breeders following a planned programme. At the present time there has been a great proliferation of 'me too' cultivars. These are plants selected from the seed collected from plants produced by the breeding programmes of others. The Netherlands is a great centre of this sort of activity, but it also goes on in North America where many plants similar to the best-selling cultivars and obviously derived from them, can be found at garden centres.

The future

There is still a lot to be done with heuchera. Many wild species have not been tried as hybrid parents, and many interesting combinations remain to be made among the present cultivars. There is a lot of variation in vigour among the modern cultivars, and the strongest-growing should be used to produce some more adaptable hybrids. At the present time, the evolution of the group as garden plants has moved so rapidly that a lot of the older purple and silver cultivars still occupy a large part of the market, even though by modern standards they are mediocre and obsolete. Palace Purple is still one of the biggest-selling varieties, used in enormous quantities in public plantings by designers who should know better. The main reason for using Palace Purple is because it is cheap to propagate by seed, but much better forms of *H. villosa* are available from tissue culture. The time has come to replace the old plants with their long, floppy flower stalks that are often cut off by gardeners with cultivars that have flowers worthy of the beautiful foliage.

TIARELLA

Tiarellas have a much more simple breeding history. Before the mid-1980s, cultivars were derived from wild plants with unusually attractive, dark leaf patterning, such as 'Running Tapestry', or leaf shape, such as *T. c.* var. *collina* 'Excelsa', or were selected from seed-raised stocks of wild-type forms. At The Primrose Path we became interested in the various foliage forms of *T. cordifolia*, and collected outstanding local native types as well as what was available in mail-order catalogues and through seed exchanges. We made some crosses among the eastern North American forms, and found that there was excellent vigour and fertility in the hybrids. Combining a pink-flowering, clumping *collina* with a local running *cordifolia* that had heavily dark-patterned leaves produced a group of seedlings from which *T.* 'Tiger Stripe' was selected. This is a vigorous clumping form with light pink flowers and entire leaves with seasonally variable, sometimes heavy maroon markings. It won a silver medal at Plantarium '96 and a gold medal at the Netherlands Royal Society for Horticulture Exhibition in 1998.

While in Portland, Oregon, for the American Rock Garden meeting in 1988 we bought a plant of *T. trifoliata* form *laciniata* from the Collector's Nursery booth at the plant sale. This form has plain green leaves that are compound with three leaflets, each of which is in turn deeply dissected. It occurs in the typical

Tiarella trifoliata f. *laciniata* (original parent plant)

form with entire leaflets at a number of places around the Puget Sound area in Washington State (Griffiths and Ganders, 1983). At home in Pennsylvania we crossed our f. *laciniata* plant with 'Tiger Stripe' and got a group of seedlings that we called the Trifoliate hybrids since they showed the lacy, compound foliage of the western parent to various degrees. Our goal with these crosses was to move the lacy cutting of the leaves of *T. trifoliata* f. *laciniata* into a line of plants with the best characteristics of the eastern types.

The flowers and flowering habit of the Trifoliate hybrids were intermediate to the parental types, making the flowers sparser and the stems more lax and spreading than the showy, erect inflorescences of 'Tiger Stripe'.

The western parent died during the hot, humid summer of 1989, so tolerance of climatic extremes was also an issue in the hybrids we were raising. We selected an especially good Trifoliate hybrid individual, 'Filigree Lace', and back-crossed it to 'Tiger Stripe', getting a group of seedlings that had much more erect and full inflorescences and deeply cut foliage marked with maroon. The best of these, 'Martha Oliver', was introduced in 1993. At this point we combined 'Martha Oliver' with an excellent form of *T. cordifolia* var. *collina* with deeply lobed foliage and scented pink flowers. The best selection from this combination, 'Elizabeth Oliver', a cultivar with sweetly scented light pink flowers on erect 40cm (16in) long stems and beautifully patterned, lacily cut foliage, embodied everything we wanted and was introduced in 1994.

'Elizabeth Oliver' has since been combined with other especially good *collina* individuals with some interesting results. It appears that genetic control of leaf shape differs in *T. trifoliata* and *T. cordifolia*. As new hybrid combinations were made in our breeding programme, the variation in leaf shape became much more extreme than in either of the original parent types. In some plants the lobes of the leaves become narrow fingers, with the leaves sometimes cut into five separate segments. In others the central leaf lobe is greatly extended, making the leaf resemble a short sword. Expression of these exaggerated traits depends on the age of the plant and its stage of growth, so that foliage clumps of plants like 'Green Sword' will have leaves of very different shapes at the same time. A recent selection, 'Pink Brushes', has extreme vigour and flower spikes that are denser, more numerous, and longer lasting than other cultivars, although the foliage is not as exaggeratedly lobed or contrastingly coloured. We are using this in our breeding programme to bring increased vigour and 'flower-power' into the other forms.

T. trifoliata flowers for a long time in early summer, rather than in mid-spring as the eastern North American types do. In the early 1990s we became interested in extending the flowering times of our cultivars, and made some exploratory back-crosses of 'Tiger Stripe' to a *T. trifoliata* type, var. *unifoliata*, which is larger and has entire, cordate leaves. 'Summer Snow' and 'Pink Pearls' were two selections we made from these crosses, and they do flower longer, from late spring into summer, but they retain a lot of the *T. trifoliata* appearance.

In the mid-1990s we gave plants of 'Elizabeth Oliver' and other selections to Terra Nova Nurseries for evaluation and possible propagation for the wholesale market. They were not marketed, but they and plants from Eco Gardens did become the basis for Terra Nova's tiarella breeding programme. Terra Nova grew large numbers of hybrids from seed, picked out the most striking plants, and rapidly filled the market with cultivars, some admittedly very handsome. At the present time it appears that in tiarella, almost all desirable combinations of foliage shape and coloration and flower form have been made, and it is difficult to see what more can be done, other than refinements. On the other hand, some of these forms could benefit from increased vigour.

HEUCHERELLA

Heuchera and tiarella will cross to produce hybrids referred to collectively as heucherellas, an amalgam of the two parent genus names. Crosses are much more likely to succeed if the seed parent is a heuchera. Seed set is usually low, with germination rates usually being about 10–20 per cent of normal. The vigour of the seedlings is highly variable, and relatively few cultivars have succeeded in reaching the market. By spring 2005 we'd counted 26, but fewer than half of them can be considered good garden plants. We have found that success in making crosses varies greatly from one pair of parental cultivars to another (persistence in making combinations may eventually reveal more compatible parents). The major obstacle to a breeding programme for heucherella is that the hybrids are sterile, and each new selection is the endpoint of that combination. This prevents the reassortment of the parental traits in new combinations that would be interesting to see. It is possible that induction of polyploidy will eventually lead to some fertile heucherellas.

The earliest heucherella was produced by Lemoine, and was introduced in 1912 as *Heucherella tiarelloides*. It had pink flowers and was reportedly a runner, unique in

Progression in tiarella leaf shape and markings in the breeding programme at The Primrose Path. A–C wild forms:
A. *T. cordifolia* var. *cordifolia*, **B.** *T. c.* var. *collina* lobed form, **C.** *T. trifoliata* f. *laciniata*. **D–F.** early hybrids: **D.** 'Tiger Stripe',
E. Trifoliate hybrid, **F.** 'Martha Oliver'. **G–I.** later hybrids: **G.** 'Elizabeth Oliver', **H.** 'Butterfly Wings', **I.** 'Green Sword'

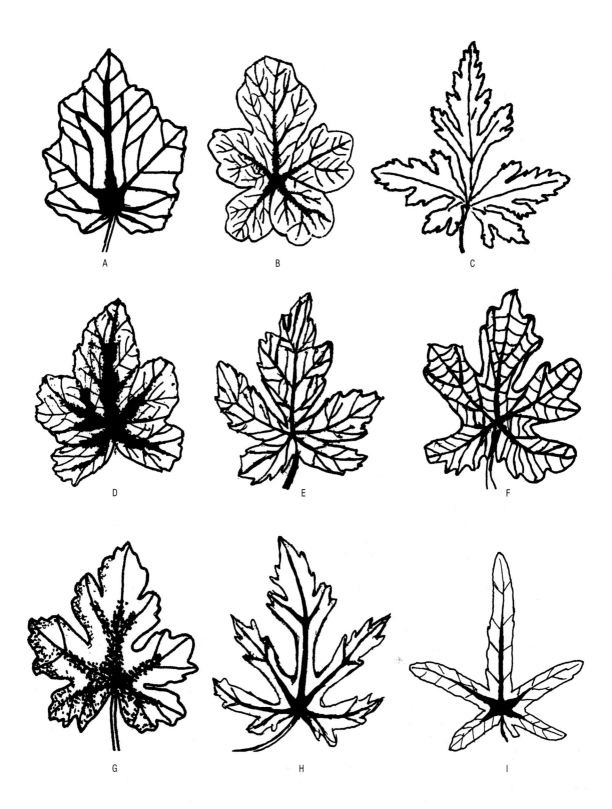

A

B

C

D

E

F

G

H

I

heucherellas. A second cultivar, *H. t.* 'Alba', a clumper with white flowers, came out in 1925. Blooms crossed *H.* 'Freedom', a pink-flowered Brizoides type, with *Tiarella wherryi* (now merged into *T. c.* var. *collina*) to get *Heucherella* 'Bridget Bloom', a form with green leaves marked with maroon, and pink and white flowers, that was introduced in 1955. 'Rosalie', bred by Tony Huber and introduced in 1983, has green leaves with a large central maroon blotch, and pink flowers.

Interested by *Heucherella* 'Bridget Bloom' and Alan Bloom's description of its origin, we tried some crosses between heuchera and tiarella at The Primrose Path in the late 1980s. The first combination was between a good pink-flowering plant chosen from a group of Bressingham hybrids, and *Tiarella wherryi*. There was good seed set, and we eventually raised about 30 healthy plants from this pairing. Two of them were selected for introduction in 1989 and named 'Tinian Pink' and 'Tinian White', 'Tinian' referring to the 18th-century land grant name of our farm. Both plants had green leaves marbled with silver, and a central maroon blotch. 'Tinian White' had white flowers, and 'Tinian Pink' pink flowers with white petals. A few years later they were given to Terra Nova for wholesale marketing and renamed 'Snow White' and 'Pink Frost', respectively.

Later heuchera x tiarella crosses were not as productive. A heuchera sibling of 'Quilters' Joy' paired with *Tiarella wherryi* produced a plant with purple and silver leaves and light pink flowers that we named 'Storm Clouds'. This grew well at first and was introduced in 1994. Our stock quickly went into decline, and the plant was dropped from later catalogues. In 1993, in response to a request by a visiting garden group to demonstrate hybrid pollination, we made the same cross again and were lucky enough to get a selection that we named 'Quicksilver' because of its highly metallic bronze and silver foliage that contrasts well with the showy, light pink

Heucherella 'Pink Frost'

flowers. This plant is probably the best heucherella that we have bred, since it is not only beautiful to look at but grows vigorously in the garden and copes well with less than ideal conditions.

In fact we have found that almost all heucherellas need pampering to grow well. Kept in a pot and fed well, they will thrive; planted in a garden with competition from other plants, they usually decline rapidly. This has limited our enthusiasm for this group of hybrids since it seems poor marketing to introduce plants that look beautiful in the sales area but are difficult to grow well.

Terra Nova began breeding heucherellas as their tiarella programme got underway. Fourteen cultivars had been introduced at the time of the listing in Dan Heims' book (2005). The best for us in western Pennsylvania have been 'Burnished Bronze' with its cut, purple-brown foliage and light pink flowers, and the handsome 'Kimono' with green, silver, and maroon leaves in the exaggerated shape of *Tiarella* 'Green Sword' and nondescript, greenish-white flowers. An obvious problem has been the small flower size, since Terra Nova has used heuchera cultivars with tiny, greenish flowers for many of the crosses. The yellow-leafed heuchera colour sports that Terra Nova has produced have been used as parents to produce yellow heucherellas such as 'Stoplight'. 'Sunspot', on the other hand, apparently arose as a somatic mutation of 'Dayglow Pink', but lacks the chlorophyll present in that plant's green and maroon foliage.

CONCLUSION

Heuchera breeding began at the end of the 19th century as an attempt to bring the general form and flower qualities of *H. sanguinea* into a vigorous plant, suitable for gardens in north-western Europe. This was accomplished by the hybridization of *H. sanguinea* with *H. americana*, *H. richardsonii* and *H. micrantha*, and by the selection of desirable hybrid plants to make the Brizoides group of cultivars. Brizoides plants were hybridized by the 1950s with *H. maxima* to produce a series of large garden hybrids at the Rancho Santa Ana Botanic Garden, and by the 1980s with small alpine species to make rock garden cultivars at the Santa Barbara Botanic Garden, and with *H. richardsonii* to make very hardy cultivars in Manitoba.

The availability of the new forms *H. americana* Dale's Strain and *H. villosa* 'Palace Purple' in the 1980s led, through *H. Montrose Ruby*, to the combination of purple-bronze and silver coloration, and the proliferation of many purple and silver cultivars through the breeding programmes of The Primrose Path and Terra Nova Nurseries. At The Primrose Path, our long-term interest in native plants, and the proximity to the large-flowered wild Appalachian species *H. pubescens* and *H. alba*, resulted in an emphasis on the development of relatively large flowers and showy foliage in our breeding programme, but the undependable hardiness of *H. micrantha* discouraged the development of cultivars with ruffled-leaves. Our emphasis on native plants in the garden also led to our breeding programme with tiarella. The milder climate of western Oregon, and the availability of selected *H. micrantha* forms, probably led to Terra Nova's interest in ruffled heucheras, especially in sports.

The modern purple and silver heuchera hybrids are essentially a new class of garden plants, and landscapers and gardeners are still learning how to use them to their best advantage. As this happens the market continues to grow, and many propagators have begun to market their own varieties derived directly from the programmes of established breeders.

6 Cultivation

HARDINESS

In general, the heuchera group is tolerant of a wide range of climatic conditions. There is a lot of variation within the group in terms of cold and heat tolerance of individual varieties, especially in the case of hybrids of complex parentage. There are also factors that affect hardiness at any given site.

The hardiest of the heucheras are the species of the americana group, especially *H. richardsonii* which has a geographic range extending far into central Canada. *H. villosa* seems to be quite hardy since even though it is from south-east North America, it grows well up into the Appalachians to at least 1920m (6300ft) (Weakley, 2005). Similarly, the small western montane species appear to be hardy in eastern North America, at least to USDA Zone 4. The weak point of the breeding programme of many of the modern heuchera hybrids has been *H. micrantha*, which has limited hardiness and heat tolerance, and hybrids with a substantial amount of *H. micrantha* inheritance can be expected to be less hardy than those without. In breeding programmes that have had little or no input of occasional wild parental material, we can also expect some loss of cold and heat tolerance as part of a general diminution of vigour due to inbreeding.

Good drainage is critical for heucheras. Planting them in heavy soil that becomes sodden in winter is fatal. Almost all of the wild species are crevice- and ledge-dwellers, and they are sufficiently hardy to be left in containers outside over winter. However, exposure to very cold, drying winds in winter can kill the crowns of heuchera, so provide shelter in open areas.

Summer heat and humidity can also cause problems with heucheras by bringing on attacks of fungus disease. The eastern species like *H. villosa*, *H. americana* and *H. pubescens* are the most resistant, and the western kinds the least. The best way to avoid this problem is to give the plants good air circulation and bright light (but not hot sun). Hybrid varieties differ greatly in their heat and humidity resistance, but those of primarily eastern parentage and high vigour are the best.

The situation with tiarellas is similar, with the eastern species very hardy and heat- and humidity-resistant, and the western much less so. Hybrid forms are probably hardy in proportion to their parentage, and those that are half *T. trifoliata* (e.g. 'Pink Pearls') will need some protection with fallen leaves, etc., where winters dive below about −15°C (5°F). All tiarellas will benefit from this sort of protection during cold winters otherwise the foliage probably won't be evergreen. Mitellas have similar needs.

The hardiness of heucherellas seems to depend on general vigour. Those plants that are not very vigorous, including the sports, have summer 'meltdown' in our garden, where temperatures can reach 32–35°C (90–95°F), and do not survive the western Pennsylvania winters.

SOIL REQUIREMENTS

The soil preferences of heucheras depend generally on the garden use categories we discussed in Chapter 2. Alpine and rock garden types grow best in lean, gritty soil of near-neutral pH. We use a mix that consists mostly of very coarse sand with some humusy loam. In nature, the wild species of this type grow in soil that consists of rock bits with decomposed plant matter.

The large species, such as *H. americana* and *H. villosa*, which enjoy woodland conditions make their best growth in neutral soil with a lot of organic matter, and selections of these species with primary hybrids like Montrose Ruby will thrive even

Heuchera 'Canyon Pink' in an attractive container at the Santa Barbara Botanic Garden, California

where there is competition with tree roots, and where the soil becomes quite dry over summer. The perennial bed types are fussier, and plants that become luxuriant in one garden often languish in others. The soil in our trialling area does not suit most heucheras. Small plants taken out of pots and put into the beds do not root out into the open soil, and eventually stop growing from lack of food and water. The soil is derived from acidic clay and shale, and has good general fertility. We have tried adding fertilizer and lime with no success, and now believe that some factor is repressing root growth. Adrian Higgins, a garden writer for the *Washington Post*, reported (column of July 29, 2004) a similar effect in his garden.

The best heuchera growth that we have seen has been in very sandy soil derived from the lake bottom in Michigan, and the sea bottom in the Netherlands, and in clay soil containing limestone chips in eastern Pennsylvania. We are now making raised, enclosed beds consisting of about 80 per cent coarse sand and 20 per cent compost with much better results. We keep the soil at a pH of 6.5–6.8, and feed the plants with a scattering of 5–10–10 slow-release fertilizer in the spring as growth starts. In gardens with soil that suits heucheras, they will still appreciate good soil preparation and feeding. We have had similar results with heucherellas. Tiarellas and mitellas, on the other hand, mostly require that the soil contain a high percentage of humus, and a good supply of food.

It has been our experience that, when local building contractors finish a house site, they flatten the soil with heavy machinery. Companies that landscape the grounds are interested in quick preparation of the site for trees and shrubs, and they then spread a heavy layer of shredded bark over the compacted soil. The mulch is highly acid and, if the soil underneath is clay, it becomes waterlogged.

A raised crevice bed.

The use of a plastic weed barrier can make the soil even more airless and dead. This sort of preparation is completely unsuitable for heucheras and most other perennials.

When a site has been mistreated in this way, rake off the mulch and improve the soil by tilling and adding sand and ground limestone. Sometimes it is best to add topsoil to raise the bed above the surrounding area. Bark and wood-chip mulches are only suitable for the woodland heucheras, heucherellas and tiarellas, and then only if they are well-rotted and not highly acidic. Rock garden and container plants should be given a mulch of pea-gravel to protect the surface of the soil, while facilitating good drainage around the plant crowns.

RAISED BED AND CONTAINER GROWING

Compared to other montane plants from western North America, the alpine heucheras are easy to cultivate in other climates. These plants have a natural affinity for rock crevices and will grow best in fast-draining sandy or gravelly soil. The alpine types do need good air circulation, and are best suited to sites that are raised up, such as the top of a wall or a special enclosed bed or container. The larger rock-garden types are suited to growing in large containers and raised beds.

Troughs are popular growing containers for alpines, and can be seen at most botanic gardens. They are essentially boxes made of a lightweight concrete mix that has had perlite or peat moss added in place of much of the gravel and sand. These are easily and cheaply constructed with instructions given in many books and by specialist societies. Heucheras, such as the smallest forms of *H. rubescens* and the Canyon hybrids, fit well in small troughs, and fill spaces between rocks with foliage that flows out over the edge of the trough. Less elegant than troughs, but still attractive, are containers such as wide clay tile drainpipes (used at the Utrecht Botanic Garden in the Netherlands), half barrels, wooden boxes and so on. The likes of wheelbarrows need something more flamboyant, like petunias and scarlet sage.

Czech plantsmen such as Josef Halda have promoted the building of crevice beds for alpines. These are mounds 1m (3½ft) or so high, made of relatively flat rocks set vertically so that there are pockets and crevices perhaps 2cm (¾in) wide and 30cm (12in) or more deep, which are filled with a soil mix suitable for alpines. Built on a level site, the crevice bed becomes a miniature 'hogback' of the sort often seen in the Appalachian shale barrens, or in the mountains of the West. If the mound is lined up east–west, then there will be north and east faces for small heucheras, and south and west faces for plants that love to bask in hot sun.

A good construction method for this sort of bed is to raise the whole thing up by making a thigh-high wall from solid concrete blocks, and filling in the container with soil, sand, and rocks. There are types of block available that are attractive, especially if the blocks that are wider at the front than the back, and which are made for curved walls, are used for the whole top course so that pockets are made for plants that will cascade down the wall. A crevice bed can be built within this raised bed.

Garden berms are often seen in North America, although they are usually haphazardly planted with shrubs and heavily mulched with shredded bark. Probably they are a way of disposing of excess soil left after a house construction. This sort of structure, a long low mound 1m (3½ft) or so high and wide, could also make a raised bed for heucheras and other perennials needing good drainage, if the soil mix is right.

LIGHT EXPOSURE

In our gardens in western Pennsylvania there is great variation in how well plants cope with full sun, but in general the green-leafed plants and those with heavier-textured bronze foliage fare best (maybe the darker coloration absorbs more heat). In areas like south-east and south-west North America, probably all varieties need protection from hot sun, but in the Pacific Northwest and northern Europe, no doubt all can be grown in sun.

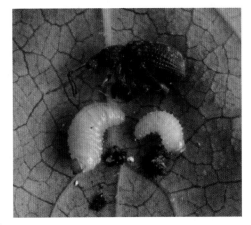

Black vine weevil adult and larvae

Alpine types in the rock garden can be planted so that they are shaded by rocks, or are placed on a north slope. While planting in heavy shade may work for *H. villosa* and *H. americana*, it's not such a good idea for the hybrid cultivars. The other genera do best in light shade. Tiarellas will grow in heavy shade but probably will not flower well, especially if the shade is from buildings or evergreens and is constant over the growing season, rather than being caused by deciduous trees.

PESTS AND DISEASES

Plants growing under favourable conditions in the garden usually are not much bothered by pests or diseases. It is when large numbers of plants are grown in pots in enclosed conditions that problems appear. The worst pest is *Otiorhynchus sulcatus* (black vine weevil), which is also a serious pest with rhododendron, yew, hemlock, grape vines and many other plants. The weevils are common in any well-established gardens. The adults can be seen walking around on the plants at night in June and July, and they lay eggs at the base of the plant. They feed on the leaves of many plants and make crescent-shaped scallops in the leaves of heuchera and related genera, epimedium and rhododendron. The larvae bore into the crowns of the plants and, when they are mature in early autumn and the

Crevice beds at Utrecht Botanic Garden, Netherlands

following spring, the plants wilt as their tops separate from the roots.

The tops can be potted up and will grow new roots as long as they are not too dehydrated, and do not contain weevil larvae. Plants that wilt in late summer can be checked for weevils by tugging at their tops to make sure that they are firmly connected to the roots. If they pull away from the roots, dig around in the soil and kill the larvae. For long-term control, nematodes can be added to the soil. Insecticides should prevent infestation if dug in around the plants in the spring before the adults are active, but they will not kill grubs already feeding within the plant crowns.

Unfortunately, weevil larvae are very often found in potted plants that are bought from garden centres, especially if they are large plants that have been there through the spring. It is worthwhile unpotting large purchased plants after they have finished flowering, and checking for weevils. Because they feed on a wide variety of plants, including shrubs, there

will always be some in nurseries. The closely related *Otiorhynchus ovatus* (strawberry root weevil) can cause similar problems.

Mealybugs can also infest heucheras. These whitish insects resemble large plant lice and cluster on the base of the plant, sucking juices. They may be protected by ants which cover the colony with a light layer of soil and, in return, 'milk' the insects for honeydew, a sweet secretion. Mealybugs can be killed by squirting with a spray bottle of soap solution. Another type of mealybug lives underground, infesting the roots. It can build up to large numbers in potted plants, but is usually kept under control by naturally occurring soil fauna in the open garden. An insecticide drench is probably the only remedy other than removing each plant from the pot and dipping it into soap solution. We have not found mealybugs a problem on the other genera of the heuchera group.

Slugs can definitely be a problem on heucheras and all the related genera, the plants with green foliage being affected the most.

Poison baits and traps are the usual remedies, and siting plants where the morning sun will dry the dew off quickly will help.

Rabbits and deer are a problem in our gardens only during the winter, when the evergreen foliage and crowns may be bitten off. The plants do recover the next spring but may be set back. Fencing or a large dog is the only protection that has worked for us.

Foliar nematodes may make unsightly yellow and brownish discoloured patches on tiarella leaves. Trimming off the affected leaves is probably the only thing that can be done to control this.

Also, hot, humid summer weather can cause fungus diseases and dieback of foliage, especially of alpine heucheras and the less vigorous cultivars. The best way to prevent this is to make sure that plants have good air circulation and are not overhung with vegetation, and to grow vigorous selections that don't need to be fussed over.

7 Propagation and practical breeding

PROPAGATION

The heuchera group is easily propagated, and the wild species, seed strains or experimental hybrids are easy to grow from seed. Selected individuals and named cultivars will have to be increased by division, cuttings or, in the case of professionals or dedicated amateurs, micropropagation (tissue culture).

Growing from seed

This group of plants is generally self-sterile. That is, pollen from an individual plant will not be successful in fertilizing seed from the same plant. We have heard of gardeners who, hearing that two plants were needed to obtain fertile seed, divided the original clump. But to get good seed set, we need two or more genetically different individuals. Heucheras are very good at trading pollen in the garden, and it will be difficult to keep wild species without hybridization occurring unless the species are grown in colonies in isolation with the plantings 50m (165ft) or more apart, or unless hand pollination is carried out with the seed parents being kept in an insect-free greenhouse or screened enclosure.

Hand pollination is a simple procedure, but the one problem with heucheras is the small size of the flowers and flower parts. We like to start with seed parents that were divisions potted the autumn before, and were maintained through the winter in an unheated greenhouse. Alternatively, plants of the small or medium-sized species can be dug, potted up and brought in during the spring. When the seed parents begin to flower, the stigmas are ready to receive pollen at the same time that ripe pollen appears on the anthers. On each branch of the flower panicle there is

a succession of buds opening. Usually there will be a flower just ready for pollination, with one or two fading and a group of buds that have not yet opened. We find the easiest procedure is to pick a few new flowers with ripe pollen from a plant in the greenhouse or growing outdoors, and pluck off individual stamens with a small pair of forceps. The anther is then dabbed against the stigma, and pollen is transferred. We begin by choosing and tagging an individual panicle, and working over the same set of flowers every day for four or five days. A total of 10–20 fertilized flowers will give enough seed for anyone who is not a large-scale producer; the unfertilized flowers dry up and fall off, leaving ripening seed capsules from the pollinated flowers.

The seed will be ripe in about six weeks. With heucheras we know that it's ripe because the seed capsules turn brown and split open at the top. In nature, most of the ripe seed remains in the capsule until shaken out by the wind in the autumn, and they germinate the following spring. We pick the seed capsules as they open, though, and sow the seed immediately. It should be surface-sown in pots or seed trays filled with a fine soil-less potting mix and left uncovered. Germination will occur within about 30 days, and seedlings will be ready to pot up individually by early autumn. However, both *H. grossulariifolia* and *H. hallii* require chilling before germination occurs. The sown seed containers can be put in plastic bags and stored in the refrigerator for six weeks or so, or be left in an unheated cold frame or outside over winter. Dry heuchera seed keeps well until the next season.

Tiarella seed is ripe when the seed capsules turn brown. Squeezing the little 'sugar scoops' will result in the seed rolling out. Mitella seed ripens exposed to view, and is ready to harvest when it turns black. Tiarella and mitella are best sown fresh like heuchera seed. Dry, stored seed may require one winter or more of chilling to induce germination.

Division

Plants of this group with a clump-forming growth pattern produce offsets at the base of the original crown. At the end of the second season the offsets begin to make their own root systems, and after the end of the third season the whole clump can be dug up in early spring, most of the soil knocked off and the clump divided into pieces and replanted.

Another method is to wait until the autumn of the second season of growth, when the rooted offsets can be pulled from the sides of the old crown without digging up the clump. They will have to be potted and kept over winter in a greenhouse or cold frame before planting out. In the case of the small mat-forming heucheras, it is easy to pull rooted rosettes from the edge of the mat and pot them up. Plants that produce runners will have rooted offspring ready to remove by late summer or early autumn.

Cuttings

Offsets without roots can be removed from old crowns in the spring and treated as cuttings. They root quickly and easily without hormone treatment in pots or seed trays filled with potting soil, and are covered by a clear plastic hood or lid to keep in the warmth and humidity.

The offsets develop from axial buds where the leaves join the main stem of the old crown. If the leaves are carefully removed with the axial bud and a little old stem tissue attached, they can be rooted like cuttings. The stolons of a running tiarella can be cut into sections, each with its own little plant, and treated as cuttings. The plantlets should be positioned so that the bases, where the roots will form, are in contact with the soil.

Micropropagation (tissue culture)

Gardening books tend to treat tissue culture as something arcane that may be important to commercial perennial production sometime in the future. In reality, the great majority of hybrid heucheras, heucherellas and tiarellas sold in North America and Europe are produced by tissue culture, and there is nothing mysterious about the method.

Strictly speaking, tissue culture is growing cells from specialized tissues, such as animal organs or plant bud meristem, under sterile conditions in the laboratory, whereas plant micropropagation usually involves growing and multiplying what are essentially tiny cuttings resembling miniature plants without roots. With some plants, micropropagation starts with tissue culture and, for a few (e.g. orchids), this can be done with single cells, but for the heuchera group the standard practice is to begin with whole growth buds or relatively large pieces – 3–4mm (0.1–0.14in) long – of the petiole base. They will produce tiny plants for multiplication a few weeks after being put into culture.

When we have decided to propagate a new plant in our tissue culture laboratory at The Primrose Path, we use an individual that has been grown in the greenhouse for at least several months. Plants brought in directly from outside have such a load of dust and fungi spores caught in their crevices and hairs, that it is almost impossible to get them clean enough to start a culture. Ideally, we'll use a plant that is just beginning to flower. At the base of the bracts on the flower stem there are axillary buds that will produce plant shoots in culture, and the fast growth rate of the inflorescence means that these parts of the plant will be relatively clean.

If a new inflorescence is not available, we'll use petiole bases from new leaves. We carefully remove whole leaves from the crown, pulling down and sideways so that the petiole base with the stipules (ear-like structures on either side) comes away whole with the growth bud at its base.

axillary bud

axillary bud

Location of buds under bracts at branch axils

We like to start 30–40 explants (plant pieces) consisting of flower stem bract bases with a small piece of stem attached, or petiole bases sliced in half with growth buds. Ragged tissue is trimmed away, and the explants are then washed successively in chlorine bleach solutions of various strengths, 70 per cent isopropyl alcohol, and sterilized distilled water to remove or kill fungi spores and bacteria. Next, the cleaned explants are placed on a nutrient medium in test tubes and left to begin growth for several weeks. It's soon obvious which explants were not successfully cleaned because they are overwhelmed and poisoned by luxuriant mould and bacteria growth in the culture tubes. Getting healthy explants started in culture can be one of the hardest parts of micropropagation. The clean explants that are starting to form cultures are referred to as TC Stage I.

The nutrient medium for the heuchera group consists of a solution of mineral salts, sugar, vitamins and growth hormones in a gel

Tiarella plantlets in TC culture container

HEUCHERA MICROPROPAGATION MEDIUM (AFTER KITTO *et al*, 1990)

Per litre
Linsmaier & Skoog Basal Medium
[= 'MS Salts'] 4.4g
Sucrose 30g
BA 0.5mg
NAA 0.025mg
Agar 6mg

Adjust pH to 5.7 with sodium hydroxide and heat until clear (just before boiling). Pour into culture vessels (about 66ml/pint jar) and autoclave for 30 minutes at 121°C (250°F).

from them. After six weeks or longer, depending on the rate of plant growth, the medium has lost its nutrients and is heavily loaded with waste product, and the plantlets must be moved to new containers. We use a medium including the hormone BA (6-benzylaminopurine), a cytokinin and a small amount of NAA (1-naphthaleneacetic acid), an auxin. The BA promotes cell and shoot formation, while the NAA fine-tunes the shoot formation. Plants at this stage, referred to as TC Stage II, grow as mounded clumps of shoots that can be removed from the culture containers every three to five weeks, divided with sterile forceps and scalpel into pieces with a few shoots each, and put onto the new medium. Our basic culture container is a pint canning jar. They are inexpensive to acquire but last virtually forever. Autoclavable plastic lids can be purchased to go with the jars. Culture containers are opened only in the laminar flow hood, an open-fronted box with a continuous flow of sterile air from back to front that allows the plantlets to be divided

made of agar, a substance derived from marine algae. The agar is firm enough to support the growing plants, yet liquid enough to allow the nutrients to travel to the plantlets and the metabolic waste products to be carried away and moved into new containers without contamination. People working in the hood need to know they should minimize the chances of contamination with their hands and instruments.

We expect a multiplication rate of about 10 every four weeks. Much higher rates are possible, but we try to use only the best-growing shoots for multiplication. At this rate it would, in theory, be possible to make one plantlet into a trillion (10^{12}) in one year.

When it is time to get the plantlets to root in order to bring them out of culture and into pots, most plants require a medium with a root-inducing hormone, or auxin. The heuchera group will produce roots as soon as cytokinin is absent, so we use a medium with no added hormone as our rooting medium. When placed in the rooting medium, tiny shoots from the clumps soon resemble miniature, mature plants, with normal crowns and leaves and a fringe of roots growing into the agar as though it were soil. These plants, TC Stage III, can be decanted from the containers and potted up. Since it takes time to produce protective waxy cuticle on the foliage, the plants must be protected from drying up for a couple of weeks. A clear plastic dome or a mist system used for cuttings does the job.

We sell mature TC Stage III plants for wholesale production, or send them out as trial plants to prospective producers in places where agricultural restrictions make it difficult to import plants in pots. We root plantlets in 350ml (12 fl oz) autoclavable polypropylene delicatessen containers with a layer of rooting medium made firmer than usual with a little extra agar. The containers with growing plants are easy and cheap to ship.

Cultivars differ greatly in how well they grow in tissue culture. Some plants tend to grow slowly or as deformed plantlets with poorly developed leaves. Others are difficult to get to root well and tend to die when potted up. In general, the plants that are the most vigorous under garden conditions will also be vigorous in culture, but that is not always the case. One of the traits that we are aiming in our new selections is ease of culture, since slow, difficult growth and high potting losses make production less dependable and more expensive.

Most of the equipment used in plant tissue culture has been adapted from other areas of laboratory science. Flow hoods were for assembling delicate electronic components in a clean atmosphere; the scalpels and forceps are general laboratory equipment; and the culture containers are really for food storage. Amateurs who are good at DIY should not find it too difficult to put together micropropagation equipment that will work well enough to grow some heuchera group plants, and there is advice about this and 'kitchen culture kits' for sale on the Web.

Tissue culture mutations

Living things grow by cell division and enlargement. When cells divide there are often genetic mistakes that produce abnormal cells. In humans those that survive to form, for example, skin tissue, almost always make benign clusters of cells such as freckles or moles. This happens in plants, too, and when there is rapid cell division in an incubator-like environment such as a tissue culture container, many abnormal cells survive to form plantlet tissue. This is often visible as oddly pigmented or twisted leaves. Abnormal plantlets can be picked out and cultured on, and this has been the source of most of the new oddly variegated heuchera cultivars. Usually variegation is not a trait that is inherited from parents by seedlings but, occasionally, whole plantlets are deficient in inheritance of pigment, and this trait gets passed on. This can result in the formation of a breeding line of plants with yellow or chartreuse foliage, as we have seen in the case of *Heuchera* 'Amber Waves' (page 38).

Induction of polyploidy

Tissue culture can also be used as part of the procedure for inducing polyploidy. This refers to a multiplication of the chromosomes to, say, twice the normal number usually found in the cells of the plant tissue. Sexual cells like pollen and unfertilized eggs have a haploid number of chromosomes, referred to as the base number, n. In the heuchera group this is 7. Non-sexual plant tissues, such as foliage and stems, formed from a union of pollen and egg that produced a seed embryo and grew into a mature plant, are normally diploid, with 2n. These cells continue to reproduce themselves in tissue culture, doubling the number of chromosomes, matching the two sets up, and apportioning a complete, diploid set of chromosomes to each daughter cell as cell division occurs. Certain chemical agents, such as colchicine, can be used to prevent cell division after chromosome doubling has occurred. When a chemical of this kind has been added to the tissue culture medium, the result can be the formation of clusters of polyploid cells that produce polyploid plantlets.

Usually cells that are polyploid are larger than normal, diploid cells. This results in polyploid plants having larger leaves and flowers. Plant breeders have used polyploidy induction to produce tetraploid (4n) daylilies, iris, amaryllis and other ornamentals (Callaway and Callaway, 2000). In most genera the breeder can tell if polyploid induction has been successful by comparing the size of stomatal guard cells (cells that open and close the tiny pores on the under surface of the leaf), or pollen grains of normal and treated plants. In heuchera these do not differ appreciably in size, but polyploidy can be detected by the technique of flow cytometry, which measures the amount of genetic material in the cell.

Polyploid heuchera do have larger flowers, and there are wild populations of tetraploid *H. grossulariifolia* that use pollination agents (i.e. insects) that are different from those of their diploid counterparts (Segraves and Thompson, 1999). Terra Nova Nurseries has been working on the induction of polyploidy in heuchera and has introduced one tetraploid

cultivar, *H.* 'Chinook', with larger flowers than its diploid parent, *H.* 'Fireworks'. Using polyploidy induction as a means of breeding larger flowers seems a costly and inefficient method to us. In addition, when tetraploid cultivars are crossed with their diploid relatives, the progeny are triploid (3n) and sterile, since there will be one set of chromosomes with no matching set. This will make it impossible to make polyploid breeding lines unless tetraploid x tetraploid crosses are used.

PRACTICAL BREEDING

Philosophy of breeding

Anyone who undertakes a breeding programme with the aim of doing more than making random crosses to see what happens must assume that there are some sort of aesthetic goals that can be visualized and described, and that the breeding programme can be a progression toward those goals. All of this depends on human value judgments since the combinations of traits found in wild plants are already highly desirable, enabling the plants to survive in nature, and any 'improvements' that we make are bound to be detrimental in any other way than survival in a garden. Obviously, these aesthetic goals are not the same for everyone since gardeners have a great range of preferences in the sorts of plants they like. On the other hand, many of them are shared, as shown by the similar goals of most of the breeding programmes we discussed in Chapter 5. Practical goals that include developing plants for special climates or breeders' interests in mutations or wild species make the programmes different.

We generally view our gardens from at least several metres away, and individual plants from arm's length to get an overall view of the traits that we have been aiming at. For example, one inflorescence might be more attractive than another because it seems fuller and better-shaped. But on close examination what this may really mean is the following:

that in the better plant the branches of the flower panicle begins lower down on the stem; that there are more panicle branches and that they are spaced more closely together; that there are more flower buds per panicle branch and more flowers open at the same time; and that the flowers are larger with a more open shape, being held at a more consistent angle. Or the foliage of one plant may be fuller and more pleasing than that of another. This effect may be caused by differences in petiole length, the number of leaves, leaf size and so on. Other overall impressions of colour, texture and so on are similarly made up of the small traits that are directly affected by the genetics of the plant.

Each of these small traits can be given a numerical rating according to how good we think it is. By doing this we have come up with a rating system for heuchera, with points ranging from 1 (poor) to 5 (excellent) for small traits such as flower size, flower colour and so on, and for traits like overall proportions. Some traits have their score doubled because they seem more important to us, and there's a possible total score of 100. As we see more clearly what more can be accomplished in enhancing some traits, one plant's score may change from one year to the next. So, last year's 4 points for flower size may be worth only 3 this year, and a plant that had a high score ten years ago may seem mediocre or poor now. Similar rating systems could be made up for tiarellas and heucherellas.

The plants that we select with this sort of rating system can be thought of as clusters of desirable traits that happened to have occurred together. When we are planning our breeding programme we are trying to increase the likelihood of the good traits clustering together. The knowledge that we have gained about how traits combine, and the ancestry of the plants we are using as parents, are crucial for our planning. Each plant is like a closed, decorated box – we see the expressed traits on the surface, but the potential that is carried in the genetic material inside can only be guessed at through our knowledge of its ancestry, and

by studying the variation in individuals from the same lot of hybrids.

Deciding which individuals to select and introduce as named cultivars is based largely on the possession of a very good rating for desirable physical traits, and on the degree of difference between this and other cultivars on the market. Heuchera group marketing has suffered from the introduction of far too many similar cultivars in the last decade, perhaps in an attempt by certain producers to saturate the market. This has led to an attitude of 'Oh no, not another heuchera' among some gardeners, although many of them are willing to pay a high price for the latest hemerocallis that has

RATING SYSTEM FOR TRIAL HEUCHERA

A. Foliage
1. Leaf.coloration (intense vs. washy hues)
2. Foliage proportions and leaf shape
3. Foliage density (fullness of clump)
4. Winter appearance

B. Flowers
1. Size x 2
2. Shape
3. Clearness of colour
4. Colour contrast with buds and stems
5. Presentation in panicle (spacing and angle of branches)
6. Proportions of inflorescence
7. Abundance of flowers
8. Length of flowering time

C. Overall
1. Overall proportions
2. Match of flowers and foliage colour
3. Vigour x 2
4. Novelty or improvement on similar forms x 2
5. Adaptability to poor conditions (hot sun, drought, sterile or acid soil)

been added to the 45,000 named cultivars already in existence. Perennial nurserymen talk about a '10ft rule', meaning that it should be possible to tell cultivars apart at this distance. This seems reasonable. While an excessive number of *H.* Brizoides cultivars were introduced during the 20th century, the dust has now settled and what we hope are the best are still on the market. Presumably, this will happen again in the 21st century with the new cultivars.

The breeding programme

With our goals in mind, we choose prospective parents each season and try to visualize what will happen if their traits are combined. Knowing where the desirable traits have come from (Chapter 4) is very useful, since similar-looking traits coming from plants that do not seem to be closely related may be due to different genes, and result in the kind of exaggerated expression that has been very important in the development of new garden plants.

Some plants make much better parents than others in terms of flower structure, allowing easy pollination, or having the tendency to produce abundant pollen or to set seed, and using these plants is clearly advantageous. Some individuals are much more likely to self-pollinate than others, and using these as seed parents will mean that the stamens will have to be removed (emasculation) before the pollen ripens on

Production fields of *Heuchera* 'Silver Scrolls' in The Netherlands

flowers that will be used for crosses. Even with our planning, the results of hybrid crosses are still highly unpredictable (and that's when the history of the breeding lines is well known), but often it is these unexpected combinations that send us in new and productive directions.

One of the basic rules in plant (or animal) breeding is that when two significantly different plants are crossed to produce first generation hybrids (an F1), the traits of the parents are combined. But F1 hybrids often fail to express the desirable traits for which the parents were chosen. When the F1 hybrids are crossed to make an F2 generation, the traits recombine and segregate out, and it's at this stage that most of the selection for desirable traits takes place. Back-crossing to one parental type or the other brings out the traits from that side. (It's important that amateur breeders become familiar with basic genetics and keep records of what they are doing. Many 'hobbyists' that we have encountered seem to be making crosses at random, and mixing their stocks together so that no one will ever be able to see where their sometimes excellent new plants have come from.)

As described earlier, we use potted seed parents kept in a greenhouse and transfer pollen to their flowers either from other potted plants or from plants growing outside. Each hybrid cross is given a code number consisting of the plant group (Heuchera) and year, followed by the number of the cross in the sequence of those made that year (e.g. H05-12) The pollinated panicle of flowers is marked with a coloured twist-tie, since different panicles can be used for different crosses. In this way the large number of small flowers in the heuchera group is an advantage. The number of the cross is recorded with the date, the parents and the tag colour. We do about 20 hybrid crosses a year, and harvest a couple of hundred seeds from each cross.

When all of the seed from a cross is ripe, we sow it in 12.5cm x 17.5cm (5 x 7in) seed trays. The germination success of heuchera hybrids is usually no more than half that of seed collected from species in the wild. We transplant hybrid seedlings during the late autumn and early winter into 6cm (2½in) pots, and keep them in a cool greenhouse. Many will flower the next spring. Seedlings with obviously undesirable traits are culled from this group, and the remainder are planted out in trial beds in the late spring and early summer. They should all flower well the following spring, and this is when the main selection is made. We then leave plants in the beds for another year to make sure that nothing outstanding has been missed, and then clear out the bed for the next batch.

We plant out about 1200 plants in the trialling area each year. From these about a dozen will be interesting enough to move to a secondary trialling area where they can be grown on and compared with cultivars already on the market. Our selection of desirable plants from the trial beds is based on the sort of criteria shown in the rating system table on page 148. Of the dozen, three or four will be put into tissue culture to test for good growth in culture, and to make enough stock for trialling by wholesale producers.

We try to keep a photographic record of the selected plants by taking pictures of the whole plants, and by scanning in portions of the flower panicles and leaves using a flat-bed scanner. However, heuchera group plants are difficult to photograph well. Not only are the parts of the plant in different planes, but the fine sprays of flowers are often lost in the background. In addition, the light-coloured flowers and reflective leaves make these parts of the plant overexposed with automatic cameras. We therefore use a digital camera with manual controls, and shoot over a wide range of exposures from the camera-recommended to the underexposed. We also try to photograph in light shade and use a background made of black felt mounted on a foam panel. In underexposed photographs the felt makes a smooth matt surface that shows off the plant well. When we try to interest producers in plants, the first thing they want to see is a photograph, and it is well worth going to a lot of trouble to get good ones.

BRINGING NEW CULTIVARS TO MARKET

After the decision has been made to introduce a selection, a couple of years of further steps have to be taken before the plant is actually available for sale. We market most of our plants through larger wholesalers, who pay us royalties for propagation rights. These nurseries need to trial plants for at least a year in their own test gardens before committing to production. They want to evaluate the plant for good growth and flowering in their climate, see whether the plant looks attractive in a pot, and whether it will fit in with the rest of their product line. We put new cultivars into tissue culture in our own laboratory, and raise a hundred or so plants that can be given out for trials.

Companies trialling our plants make a trialling agreement with us, which states, among other restrictions, that the trialling nursery will not use the plants in its own breeding programme. Even so, we avoid giving plants to nurseries that produce their own heuchera and tiarella cultivars because, from past experience, we believe that our trial material will inevitably manage to sneak its genes into their breeding stock. When the trialler has agreed to propagate and market our plant, that will have to be protected by a patent or some other kind of breeder's rights, we make an agreement licensing propagation and marketing, and stating the geographic marketing region and royalty.

By this point we need to find a name for our new plant. A good name is important, and choosing one is sometimes very difficult. A name can be almost anything that has not been used before, consisting of no more than three or four words. For Plant Variety Rights applications (or the plant patent), the European Union insists that names have a noun instead of just consisting of adjectives, i.e. 'Beautiful One' rather than 'Beautiful Blue'. In North America the patents need to be filed within a year of the plant being offered for sale. Since 'offered for sale' can be construed to mean pictured and/or discussed in a magazine article, or displayed at a nurserymen's convention, we are careful to keep information confidential up to the actual time of market release.

In the USA, plant patents can be very expensive (up to $15,000) if all the work is done by a patent attorney. This consists of compiling plant measurements and providing information on growth under controlled conditions, comparing the plant to other, similar forms on the market and to the parental forms, and providing photographs to the Patent Office's specifications. But by working with a patent agent instead of an attorney, and providing photographs and all other data ourselves, we are able to get our costs down to about $2700 per patent at the present time.

When the licensed producer is writing catalogue copy listing our new plant, he will demand gorgeous photographs that will make the plant irresistible to the wholesale buyer and that they can use to sell to their retail customers. We make a point of offering photos and copy free for marketing use.

It is very satisfying to bring new plants onto the market, especially if they are well received by the gardening public. It is always a pleasure for us to see our plants at garden centres and to hear appreciative comments about them.

8 Where to see heucheras and related plants

PUBLIC GARDENS

It is surprising to us how few public gardens choose to grow a good selection of heucheras and tiarellas. We hope this will soon change. These are a few of the gardens that particularly impress us.

Cambridge University Botanic Garden

Cory Lodge, Bateman Street, Cambridge
CB2 1JF
Tel: 01223 336 265
email: enquiries@botanic.cam.ac.uk
www.botanic.cam.ac.uk
The garden has a good collection of species heucheras in the rock garden, which has heucheras between the large stones.

Royal Botanic Garden, Edinburgh

20A Inverleith Row, Edinburgh EH3 5LR
Tel: 0131 552 7171
email: info@rbge.org.uk
www.rbge.org.uk
An excellent collection of western North American species heucheras, and some of the older Brizoides varieties. They have a searchable database on their website that shows the bed where any given plant is growing in the garden.

Rancho Santa Ana Botanic Garden

1500 North College Avenue
Claremont, CA 91711-3157, USA
Tel: 001 909 625 8767
email: Ann.Joslin@cgu.edu
www.rsabg.org
Large displays of the Rancho Santa Ana hybrid heucheras and *H. maxima*, one of their parents. The masses of plants are very impressive, but the style is probably not easily translatable to a small, private garden.

Santa Barbara Botanic Garden

1212 Mission Canyon Road, Santa Barbara, CA 93105, USA
Tel: 001 805 563 0352
Email: info@sbbg.org
www.sbbg.org
Displays its Canyon hybrids and some of the Rancho Santa Ana hybrids in a variety of settings, from small beds of one cultivar to mixed plantings and containers.

The University of Georgia

111 Plant Sciences Building, Department of Horticulture, University of Georgia, Athens, GA 30602, USA
Tel: 001 706 542 2471
ugatrial.hort.uga.edu
The University of Georgia does extensive perennial trials. The results are posted at the end of each season on their website. They grow the plants well and are well worth visiting. There are other public gardens in North America that conduct perennial trials, but you have to buy a publication to see the results which doesn't exactly make it accessible, and it is not much of a service to the gardening public.

Fernwood Botanical Garden and Nature Preserve

13988 Range Line Road, Niles, MI 49120, USA
Tel: 001 269 695 6491
www.fernwoodbotanical.org
Fernwood's special feature is a 5-acre tall grass prairie where *Heuchera richardsonii* can be seen in a natural setting.

NATURAL PLACES

Most of the mountainous parts of North America have heuchera species that are common and easily found. Tiarellas and mitellas are less widespread, but on a walk through the forest in the Appalachians or the mountains along the Pacific Coast one is sure to see the local species. In the 21st century it is not difficult to track down sites for specific plants, since there are inventory lists on the Web for many state parks and natural areas. The Forests of the Central Appalachians Project Web site (http://asecular.com/forests), with text and photographs by Robert F Mueller, is an example of the invaluable information that can be found on the Internet.

There are some memorable places where we have seen wild heucheras, tiarellas and mitellas. They are worth visiting because they are outstanding botanical and scenic localitions, but they are also good examples of the sorts of places where these plants thrive. We once hiked in the mountains of West Virginia in mid-June and the Oregon Cascades in late June, and were interested to see the same plant genera (but different species) growing in the same habitats in the two places. This is true also of the heuchera group: becoming acquainted with their habitats in one geographic area will allow you to find the right habitats in other places thousands of miles way.

At Ohiopyle State Park, Fayette County, Pennsylvania (www.dcnr.state.pa.us/stateparks/parks/ohiopyle.aspx), the Great Gorge Trail is an easy walk along the hillside above the Youghiogheny River, which runs through a steep gorge over a series of rapids. The trail is through rich, deciduous forest with the most diverse range of wildflowers that we have seen in Pennsylvania. Near the first bridge over a stream there is a particularly good colony of *Tiarella cordifolia*, many plants with maroon markings on the foliage, and there are large and showy individuals of *Mitella diphylla*. The plants are in flower between about 25 April and 10 May. Along the Youghiogheny Bike Trail, north of Ohiopyle, there are limestone cliffs with *Heuchera americana* growing in the crevices, often in deep shade. The plants are greatly reduced in size, but the seed produces individuals of normal size when grown in our garden.

Greenland Gap Preserve, Grant Co., West Virginia(nature.org/wherewework/northamerica/states/westvirginia/preserves/art1203.html) has the most spectacular heuchera site we have seen in eastern North America. The road along the stream passes through forest in a narrow canyon in the mountains, and then briefly emerges into the open where a large rockslide has come down the cliffs. Growing on and between the blocks of sandstone, as if in an enormous rock garden, are *H. pubescens*. These plants are in full light, albeit on a north-facing slope, and are the most luxuriant and showy individuals we have seen. There are also *Rhododendron maximum* and *Polypodium virginianum* (polypody fern) on the rocks. The soil is a mixture of rock chips and peaty humus, and has a pH of 6.4, surprisingly near neutral for thriving rhododendrons. At Trough Creek State Park in Huntington County, Pennsylvania, there are also good displays of *Heuchera pubescens* on the rocks and ledges along the road that skirts Raystown Lake. Mid-June is a good time to see the plants in flower.

Spruce Knob, Pendleton County, West Virginia(www.fs.fed.us/r9/mnf/sp/spruce_knob.html) is the highest mountain in the state. The summit is at about 1480m (4900ft), and can be reached on a good forest service road. There are spectacular views down into the valleys on either side. The vegetation at the summit consists mostly of ericaceous shrubs and dwarf spruce trees, and the soil is peaty and acid. This is one of the best places to see *H. alba* in the wild. There is a large colony among the sandstone rocks to the right soon after the road to the summit emerges from the forest. The plants grow mostly in protected spots among the rocks, and look very much like western North American alpines in growth habit, which will come as a surprise to gardeners used to the tall inflorescences of tiny flowers of easterners like *H. americana* and *H. villosa*. Many of the western species grow in similar sites. Early July is when *H. alba* flowers, unfortunately too late for the abundant deciduous azaleas.

Mary's Peak, in the Coast Range west of Corvallis, Oregon (www.maryspeak.org), is a famous botanical location, with a good road that goes almost to the summit, 1260m (4,150ft) high. Along the road, about two-thirds of the way to the top, there is a small waterfall with a wet, shady cliff to one side. Here, in the crevices, are lush plants of *H. micrantha*. Near the top of the mountain is a car park among montane meadows, and just above this a natural rock garden at the summit. Along the trail in the woodland at the bottom of the car park you'll find *Tiarella trifoliata* and *Tellima grandiflora*.

The Sheep Lake Trail from Chinook Pass to Sheep Lake in the Cascade Mountains in Yakima County, Washington, at about 1500m (4900ft) up, passes large rocks and cliffs within a mile of the highway. In the relatively dry crevices here is *H. glabra*, growing in the same sort of site and looking very much like the dwarfed *H. americana* in rock crevices in Pennsylvania. In cracks in the cliffs above, far out of reach, are tufts of *H. cylindrica*, with reddish flower stems about 50cm (20in) long and showy white flowers. Further along the trail in coniferous forest there are three species of *Mitella*, all fairly inconspicuous and similar.

The mountains of southern California have more than their fair share of beautiful heucheras. We have not had the opportunity to see them in settings other than botanical gardens, but for those who hike in this area Tom Chester's detailed plant lists and trail descriptions are an invaluable source of information.

Charles Oliver photographs *Heuchera* 'Wendy' at the Rancho Santa Ana Botanic Garden, California

Heuchera species

(Based on the PLANTS Database – http://plants.usda.gov)

The species that have had significant use in horticulture, either as garden subjects or as parts of breeding programmes, are in bold.

abramsii (San Gabriel alum root) California; alpine

acutifolia (sharp-leafed alum root) Mexico

alba (white alum root) Central Appalachians; rock garden

alpestris (San Bernardino Mountain alum root) California; alpine

americana (American alum root) Eastern North America; naturalizing and perennial beds

amoena (pleasant alum root) Mexico

bracteata (bracted alum root) Central Rocky Mountains; alpine

brevistaminea (Laguna Mountain alum root) California

caespitosa (tufted alum root) California

caroliniana (Carolina alum root) North and South Carolina

chlorantha (tall alum root) Far western North America

cylindrica (roundleaf alum root) Western North America; alpine, rock garden

duranii (hard alum root) California and Nevada

eastwoodiae (Senator Mine alum root) Arizona

elegans (urnflower alum root) California; alpine

flabellifolia (Bridger Mountain alum root) Western North America

glabra (alpine alum root) Alaska to Oregon; alpine

glomerulata (Chiricahua Mountain alum root) New Mexico and Arizona

grossulariifolia (gooseberry leaf alum root) Western North America; alpine, rock garden

hallii (Front Range alum root) Colorado; alpine

hemsleyana (Hemsley's alum root) Mexico

hirsutissima (shaggyhair alum root) California; alpine

longiflora (longflower alum root) Central to southern Appalachians

maxima (Jill of the rocks) California; naturalizing

merriamii (Merriam's alum root) California and Oregon; alpine

micrantha (crevice alum root) Pacific northwest; rock garden

novomexicana (New Mexico alum root) Arizona and New Mexico

orizabensis (Orizaba alum root) Mexico

parishii (Mill Creek alum root) California; alpine

parviflora (little flower alum root) South eastern North America

parvifolia (little leaf alum root) Rocky Mountains; alpine

pilosissima (seaside alum root) California and Oregon; rock garden

pubescens (downy alum root) Central Appalachians; rock garden

pulchella (Sandia Mountain alum root) New Mexico; alpine

richardsonii (Richardson's alum root) Central North America; naturalizing

rubescens (pink alum root) Western North America; alpine

sanguinea (coral bells) New Mexico and Arizona; rock garden

villosa (hairy alum root) Eastern North America; naturalizing

wootonii (White Mountain alum root) New Mexico

Glossary

Anther The pollen-bearing body at the top of the stamen.

Axil The juncture of a leaf or shoot and a stem.

Axillary Found at the juncture of a leaf or shoot and a stem.

Backcross A mating of an F1 hybrid to one of the parental types.

Bract A leaf-like structure borne behind the flower or on the flower stem.

Calyx The structure outside the petals, usually bell-like or saucer-like in the heuchera group.

Caudex A persistent (i.e. perennial) basal stem.

Chimaera An organism constructed of tissues that are genetically different from each other.

Chloroplast A structure that contains photosynthetic pigment in plant cells.

Clone A group of genetically identical individuals.

Compound A leaf that is divided in separate leaflets.

Cordate Shaped like a heart.

Cultivar A selected plant clone.

Dicot Plant having two seed leaves at germination. One of the two botanical divisions of flowering plants.

Epidermis The outermost layer or skin of cells.

F1 hybrid The progeny of a cross between two individuals that differ genetically to a significant degree.

F2 hybrid The progeny of a cross between two F1 hybrids.

Hypanthium In heuchera the fused structure consisting of the lower parts of the stamens, petals, and calyx.

Inflorescence The whole flowering part of a plant.

Introduce To bring a plant onto the market.

Laciniate Cut into narrow pointed lobes.

Meristem Cells capable of growing into specialized tissues.

Monocot Plant having one seed leaf upon germination. One of the two botanical divisions of flowering plants.

Mutation A change in the genetic makeup of a cell.

Ovary The structure at the base of the flower where seeds develop.

Panicle A branched compound inflorescence.

Patterning Mottling of the leaf surface that is part of the normal, adaptive colouration of the plant.

Peduncle The primary flower stalk.

Petiole The stem of a leaf.

Polyploid Having a chromosome number that is a multiple of the usual for a species or group of species.

Sinus The recess between two leaf lobes.

Somatic Relating to the non-sexual cells of an organism.

Sport A plant individual that has unusual qualities due to a novel genetic abnormality.

Stamen The anther bearing structure of a flower.

Stigma Surface at tip of style where pollen is deposited.

Stolon A runner that roots to form a new plant.

Style Attenuated structure above the ovary which supports the stigma.

Variegation Unusual, patchy foliage colouration due to non-adaptive individual genetic abnormality.

Zygomorphic Having the calyx longer on one side than the other.

Bibliography and resources

Bloom, A, 1981. *Perennials for Your Garden.* Floraprint USA, Chicago.

Bloom, A, 1991. *Alan Bloom's Hardy Perennials: New Plants Raised and Introduced by a Lifelong Plantsman.* A & C Black. London.

Brown, B, 2002. 'Heucheras: New and Improved.' *The Garden.* August, 2002. http://www.rhs.org.uk/Learning/publications/pubs/garden0802/heucheras.asp

Burrell, C, 1999. *Perennial Combinations: Stunning Combinations that Make Your Garden Look Fantastic Right from the Start.* Rodale Books. Emmaus, PA.

Callaway, D J, and Callaway, M B eds. 2000. *Breeding Ornamental Plants.* Timber Press, Portland, OR.

Chester, T, 2004. 'Thomas Jay Chester's Website.' http://sd.znet.com/~schester/tchester/index.html

Cohen, S, and Ondra, N J, 2005. *The Perennial Gardener's Design Primer.* Storey Publishing. North Adams, MA.

Druse, K, 2000. *Making More Plants: The Science, Art, and Joy of Propagation.* Clarkson Potter, New York.

Ferrari, J, ed. 1999. *A Rock Garden Handbook for Beginners.* North American Rock Garden Society.

Foster, S, and Duke, J A, 1990. *A Field Guide to Medicinal Plants: Eastern and Central North America.* Houghton Mifflin Co., Boston and New York.

Gardner, J, and Bussolini, K, 2005. *Elegant Silvers: Striking Plants for Every Garden.* Timber Press, Portland, OR.

Glattstein, J, 2003. *Consider the Leaf: Foliage in Garden Design.* Timber Press, Portland, OR.

Griffiths, A J F, and Ganders, F R, 1983. *Wildflower Genetics: A Field Guide for British Columbia and the Pacific Northwest.* U. British Columbia, Vancouver.

Heims, D, and Ware, G, 2005. *Heucheras and Heucherellas: Coral Bells and Foamy Bells.* Timber Press, Portland, OR.

Higgins, A. 'On Again/Off Again Affair with Coral Bells.' *Washington Post*, July 29, 2004. pp. H1, H6.

Jekyll, G, 1982. *Colour Schemes in the Flower Garden*, 8th ed. Antique Collectors' Club Ltd., Woodbridge, UK

Kitto, S L, Frett, J J and Geiselhart, P, 1990. *Micropropagation and field evaluation of x Heucherella 'Bridget Bloom'.* J. Environ. Hort. 8 (3): 156–159

Klinkhamer, L, 2005. 'Luc Klinkhamer's Perennial World.' http://www.lucsperennialworld.com

Kyte, L, and Kleyn, J, 1996. *Plants from Test Tubes: An Introduction to Micropropagation.* Timber Press, Portland, OR. Third Ed.

Moran, R C, 2004. *A Natural History of Ferns.* Timber Press, Portland, OR.

Natural Resources Conservation Service. 'PLANTS Database.' 2005. http://plants.usda.gov/

North American Rock Garden Society. 1996. *Handbook on Troughs.*

Oliver, C G, 2005. 'Featured Plants from The Primrose Path.' http://www.theprimrosepath.com/Featured_Plants/index.html

Rosendahl, C O, Butters, F K and Lakela, O, 1936. *A Monograph on the Genus Heuchera.* U. Mn. Press, Minneapolis.

Royal Horticultural Society. 2005. *RHS Plant Finder 2005–2006.* Dorling Kindersley. London.

Segraves, K A, and Thompson, J N, 1999. *Plant polyploidy and pollination: floral traits and insect visits to diploid and tetraploid* Heuchera grossulariifolia. Evolution 53 (4): 1114–1127

Weakley, A, 2005. *Flora of the Carolinas, Virginia, and Georgia.* Working Draft of 10 June 2005. UNC Herbarium.

Wells, E F, 1984. *A revision of the genus Heuchera (Saxifragaceae) in eastern North America.* Syst. Bot. Monogr., Vol. 3., pp. 45–121.

Index